T0194908

# I Am a *Child*
## • • •
# I Did *Not* Ask
# to Be *Born*
# But I'm Here
## • • •

Catherine Smith Robinson, MEd

author HOUSE

*AuthorHouse™*
*1663 Liberty Drive*
*Bloomington, IN 47403*
*www.authorhouse.com*
*Phone: 1 (800) 839-8640*

*Published by AuthorHouse   12/27/2019*

*ISBN: 978-1-7283-2155-4 (sc)*
*ISBN: 978-1-7283-2154-7 (e)*

*Library of Congress Control Number: 2019911003*

*Print information available on the last page.*

*Any people depicted in stock imagery provided by Getty Images are models, and such images are being used for illustrative purposes only. Certain stock imagery © Getty Images.*

*This book is printed on acid-free paper.*

*Scripture taken from The Holy Bible, King James Version. Public Domain*

# Contents

# Acknowledgments

I would like to honor the Lord Jesus Christ for the ability to write my first book. If it had not been for him, this journey wouldn't have been completed. I give thanks to him for all of the blessings he has bestowed upon me.

Grace and honor to Michelle Washington for her obedience to God in writing the poem "I Am A Child … I Did Not Ask to Be Born But I'm Here …" She wrote it on behalf of my mission in life to save our children. God had a special purpose for it, and neither of us had a clue at the time you gave me a copy of your rough draft twenty-one years ago. I pray that this poem will always bless your life and many others.

Jackie Cleveland, my forever friend, you are my Christian sister. Motivation is one of your gifts. When you told me to stay focused, I knew that I had to keep moving forward. As you prepare for your move thousands of miles away, always remember we will be forever friends.

My special appreciation to Louise Laron for your faith in me. You believed in my gift as a first-time author and did the unexpected. Before my book was published, you purchased the first copy. Thank you for having faith in my destiny. I pray this book will be a blessing to you and to your family.

# A Tribute to My Mother

My mother was a faithful woman of God and the most beautiful and wonderful parent a child could have. My words can't express the love and care that I experienced from her love and kindness. She was a Proverbs 31 virtuous mother, and she took care of her family in excellence. Her children were so precious to her, and I have felt the power of her love each and every day of my life. My mother planted the seed of God in the hearts of her children and was a powerful advocate of education. Out of seven children, five completed college or above.

She was an awesome woman of God and an extraordinary mother. I never heard her complain. The words she spoke were words of kindness, love, and peace. She was the closest person that exemplified the character and integrity of Christ in my life. What a true blessing my mother was to me. I didn't have to look outside my home for a role model. My mother was a role model I could trust because I saw her lifestyle in living color every day. She has truly made a difference in my life.

# "I Am A Child ... I Did Not Ask to Be Born But I'm Here ..."

I am a child. I did not ask to be born, but I'm here. I need love, peace, and understanding. I need goodness, kindness, and support from those who care.

My feelings are colorless. They do not know racial boundaries. My needs are inborn. They came with me from my mother's womb.

I need to be heard.

I need to be held.

I need to be hugged.

I need to be honored without condition.

—Michelle L. Washington
Copyright 1998

# Introduction

Parenting is not an easy job. It's not for everyone! There are no real manuals for parenting; however, there are many helpful resources to assist parents with raising their children. Parenting presents many issues and concerns of life. There is a need for parents to get in deeper touch with the emotional and mental state of children. I felt this need daily working with children and parents very closely as a teacher in both private and public schools.

I am the mother of three blessed adult children Casper Jr., Crissi, and Creshawn. My awesome grandsons Bruce and Cayson are my greatest joy. The experiences raising three children made me more compassionate toward parents. Working with children and parents for almost fifty years as a teacher, minister, and a CEO of a children and youth organization, I understand the highs and lows of parenting. When I gave my heart to the Lord, I got my greatest revelation about children and parenting.

God is the creator of life, and children are extremely precious to him. He wants parents to love and nurture their children and to accept them unconditionally. Children depend on their parents for all of their needs. The Lord inspired me that parents are a very important part of the success of their children. I encouraged parents to mentor their own children.

This book is a wake-up call to parents. Children don't ask to be born. To have and raise children is a very sacrificial journey. Much prayer and deep consideration needs to be made in deciding to become a parent. Hopefully, for those who are parents, this book will serve as an alert to the sensitivity of children and their need to be accepted and loved. It is very important for parents to find ways to stay connected with their children's emotional and mental state.

# CHAPTER 1

# The Blood of America's Children

America, America, why do we continue to bury our young? Why do we continue to abort our young? Why do we continue to abuse our young? Why do we continue to kill our young? The whole earth mourns for answers to why our children are dying. Parents cry for their young. Families cry for their young. Schools cry for their young. Churches cry for their young.

Our children are dying at the hands of weapons. Children are killing their peers and parents. Parents are killing their children. America is mourning the deaths of children much too soon. Children are going to early graves. What is the problem?

Families are in a crisis in our land. We hear about it in the news on television and radio, and we read about it in the newspaper. The government can't solve the problems of our children and parents. And neither can the communities or schools.

Many churches aren't bringing solutions to hurting children and families. More emphasis appears to be on the prosperity message. Our families need healing and restoration. Who can hear the cries of the children? The blood of innocent children continues to flow throughout this nation. One of the scriptures that addresses the shedding of blood is in the book of Proverbs.

> These six things doth the Lord hate: yea, seven are an abomination unto him:
> A proud look, a lying tongue, and hands that shed innocent blood,
> A heart that deviseth wicked imaginations, feet that be swift in running to mischief,
> A false witness that speaketh lies, and he that soweth discord among brethren.
> (Proverbs 6:16–19 KJV)

**Parent Alert**

American is mourning the deaths of children much too soon. Children are going to early graves.

What is wrong with the children? They are killing each other. What is wrong with this generation? Don't they understand that they should never take someone's life? Do they value life at all? Are the children taught moral values in the home?

Today America points the finger but doesn't hear the cries of its children. As the cries get louder and louder, where are the people who hear those cries? Where are the voices that speak for the children? Can you hear the sound of the children? What are they saying? The time has come; this nation must listen. The time has come when we must speak to this generation. Silence no more!

Children are wounded. They don't really know what is happening. What they do know is that they don't want to hurt anymore. What are we doing to help this generation? We must give them hope. We must give them love. We must put our arms around them and show them that we care. After all the talk, we must be willing to do something. We can't afford to lose this generation.

Rise to the cause and make a commitment in your heart—not in your head or your mind. America, while our children are killing and slaughtering each other, we are more concerned with helping other countries win their wars. It's time for this nation to concentrate on the domestic scene. What about the children? When we don't do anything, our actions speak louder than our words. Children feel they aren't important in this country. Why do we point a finger at them for every negative thing they do? Are we sending false messages to our children? Is it that only adults have the right to make mistakes? This is one of the reasons children might not trust their parents.

**Parent Alert**

Children are wounded. They don't know what is really happening. What they do know is that they don't want to hurt anymore.

America, we are in a crisis. The nation is dying because our children are dying. Families and communities are in crisis. What is the answer? Did it start when prayer was taken out of the schools? When did it start? In my opinion, it started when family values changed. It started when prayer was taken out of the home. Families stopped praying and believing in God.

Parents sent children to church instead of attending with them. Fathers became less responsible for providing for their wives and children. Mothers left the home for many reasons. Some mothers desired a larger home, a nicer car, and more material things. As a result of divorce, other mothers had to go to work. Nevertheless, the home became empty of parents.

Babies and young children were placed in day-care centers or taken to babysitters.

Parents had less responsibility with taking care of their children. Some children had to go to the bus stop alone because parents had to go to work early. Children are crying. Can anyone hear the cries of this generation?

**Parent Alert**

Nevertheless, the home became empty of parents. Babies and young children were placed in day-care centers or taken to babysitters.

# The Cry of a Generation

The time has come to wipe the faces of our children. Parents, listen to the sounds of your children. Children are crying out for love. They aren't looking for love in all the wrong places; they are looking for it from their parents. When they can't find it there, they accept it wherever they can find it. It could be in a chat room on the internet, the sport coach, the gangs at their school, and many other places.

Many children resort to taking drugs because they don't feel loved. They're popular at school, and children seem to know how to get drugs without their parents' knowledge. Some children get high to forget about negative feelings they have about themselves. I don't believe parents want their children to substitute drugs for love. Parents, hear the cries of your children. They are cries in their spirits, and they need your help.

God has given parents the responsibility to take care of their children. He expects them to protect and love them, no matter what is going on in their lives. Listen. Can't you hear the sound? It doesn't sound like music, and it's not a good sound. It's a sound of pain and distress. You can hear the sound at home, in the schools, and all over the community. Wherever children are, you can hear the sound. The cries of children are as a rushing wind across this nation and the world.

**Parent Alert**

Children are crying out for love. They aren't looking for love in all the wrong places. They are looking for love from their parents.

## The Cry of a Generation

Listen, do you hear crying?
It's a cry for love, but they feel hate.
It's a cry of anger when resentment is near.
It's a cry of fear, and they want to be safe.
It's a cry of hopelessness, and hope is what they need.
It's a cry of wounded spirits, and the pain won't go away.
It's a cry of helplessness and a need for a helping hand.
It's a cry of rejection when acceptance is what they need.
It's a cry of neglect, wanting someone to care.
It's a cry of abuse, and the heart speaks, "Love me."
It's a cry of incest when they need loving arms to hold them.
It's a cry of home alone, and fear is all around them.
It's a cry of torment and a need for perfect peace.
It's a cry of broken hearts, and the pain won't go away.
It's a cry of a teen having a child, crying out for help.
It's a cry of homelessness and a desire to have a loving home.
It's a cry to be me. Can you love me?

—Catherine Smith Robinson

When will this nation take a stand on behalf of its children? The children in this nation need to be healed. Where are the parents? We must rise and know that change doesn't just happen. Someone has to proclaim change and then do something. Action has to be a part of the plan. What is happening to children is everybody's problem.

It is the responsibility of the parents to love, nurture, guide, train, teach, support, and provide a safe and healthy environment for their children. America, we don't need another space program or another education program such as No Child Left Behind. Our children are dying.

Some are dying physically.
Some are dying emotionally.
Some are dying socially.
Some are dying mentally.
Some are dying intellectually.
Some are dying spiritually.

In this nation, do we care more about our dogs than our children? Have we given it a thought? We walk our dogs. We talk to them. We hug and kiss them. Some people even sleep with their dogs. When is the last time you hugged your daughter or your son? And how much time do you spend with them? When is the last time you took your toddler for a walk? There is absolutely nothing wrong with owning and taking care of a dog or another pet. However, how do we view our responsibilities to our children in comparison to our pets?

## The Rejected One

The world needs love, not hate. People need to care about people, and parents need to love their children. We can't just sing and talk about love. *Love* is an action word. Children need to see and feel loved. Why are there so many rejected children in this nation? What reasons do we have to find God's little creations unacceptable?

Rejection starts in the spirit of a child and is a process of not being acceptable. It's like a seed that's planted in the heart when a child is neglected, rejected, or abused by his or her parents or someone else. If the child isn't healed from the hurts, the wound grows inside. Later, the hurt can be manifested in harmful ways. Don't let your child be named among the rejected ones in our society.

When children are not loved and cared for properly, they begin to feel rejected. They start to feel brokenhearted and need to be healed. However, if no one notices it, the hurt continues to multiply. The fear of rejection is like a wall of protection to prevent from receiving more hurts. This is a false protection, because it can open up the door of the spirit of a child to anger, unforgiveness, strife, bitterness, jealousy, selfishness, envy, rejection, low self-esteem, and deeper wounds. These risky behavior issues can lead to juvenile crime, gangs, violence, and other negative influences.

The path of rejection can begin at an early age. Look around you; there are many children who feel rejected by their parents or someone else. Their deep hurts are normally not verbally expressed. However, there can be a residue of hurt that causes them to be fearful. They grow up scared, and sooner or later the fear manifests in many ways. These risky behaviors can be a form of contentment and be satisfactory, while they only are capable of bringing destruction. Children need to be loved by their parents, and they need to know that they are loved. Every child has the right to be cared for in a stable and loving environment.

No child is an accident. Every child has a God-given purpose in life. There are mothers who wish that their children had never been born. Some children may be rejected after parents get a divorce. There are even children that were rejected in the womb and never had a chance to live. Children represent a treasure from God. Once they are born, they shouldn't have to experience rejection from their parents or anyone else. Parents, open up your hearts and your spirits and accept God's precious creations with his love.

**Parent Alert**

No child is an accident. Every child has a God-given purpose in life.

The word of God shows us that children are a blessing to parents. Joseph stated this about his sons:

> And Israel beheld Joseph's sons, and said, Who are these?
> And Joseph said unto his father, They are my sons, whom God hath given me in this place. And he said, Bring them, I pray thee, unto me, and I will bless them. (Genesis 48:8–9 KJV)

## Somebody's Crying

A new day is dawning. Parents, this isn't the time to miss the cry of the children. When is the last time you listened to your child talk? Did you tell him or her to be quiet, or did you listen patiently to what he or she had to say. A child's voice is the inner cry of the soul. It reveals what is on his or her little heart. The last time your child was angry, did you minister or counsel with him or her? What tone of voice did you display? Did you hear the sound of one who needed to be comforted and reassured? Parents, what about the children? Will you listen to their cries?

"Shhh, Somebody's Crying"

Shhhh, listen! Somebody's crying.
Can you hear the sound?
Did you answer when they called you?
Did you refuse to take the time?
Is it always about you and not your child?
Shhhh, listen! Somebody's crying.
Did you hear the sound?
It was your daughter raped by her boyfriend,
Home alone, and you didn't hear the cry.
Shhhh, listen! Somebody's crying.
Did you hear the sound?
It was your son bullied at school.
Heard the cry, but I didn't believe.
Shhhh, listen! Somebody's crying.
The children were playing outside one night.
I was cooking a late dinner and wanted
Them out of sight.
A drive-by shooting took place
And took my daughter's life.
Shhhh, listen! Somebody's crying.
I was watching my favorite TV program.
I forgot to lock the door.
I missed my toddler, and found him
In the swimming pool.
He's not crying anymore.
Shhhh, listen! Somebody's crying.
I sent my teen son to the grocery store.
He didn't have a license, but I thought it was okay.
My son didn't come back; a car accident took him away.
Shhhh, listen, somebody's crying.
I had to work tonight, and left my daughter
With my boyfriend.
He just loved to babysit my little girl.
Now she's a victim of rape. What can I say?
I couldn't hear anybody crying.

—Catherine Smith Robinson

We mourn the deaths, and the hurts of a generation. Isn't it our responsibility to hear the cry of our children? Can we listen to our children's voices, take the time, and respond to their needs? Parents are the ones to listen to their heart's cry. However, be careful that you don't wait too late.

"Don't Shed a Tear!"

Were you there when I needed you?
Don't shed a tear for me now!
I wished many days that you were there,
But you probably didn't even care.
Don't shed a tear for me now!
I wanted to hear your voice so many times.
As I cried out louder and louder to your silence,
I wanted to feel your touch, and I needed you so much.
I needed to hear you say that you loved me.
I couldn't understand why you were so busy all the time.
Don't shed a tear for me now!
I won't bother you anymore.
This world is not my home, and I don't want to come back.
I am with God now, and he takes good care of me.
So please don't worry about me anymore,
And don't shed a tear for me now!

—Catherine Smith Robinson

**Parent Alert**

Can we listen to our children's voices, take the time, and respond to their needs?

## What Child Is This?

God created children to be a blessing to their parents. The miracle of life is enough to show the love of God for the children. A tiny seed planted in the womb of a woman by a man becomes a baby. It seems that the child actually comes out of nowhere. The life of a child is truly a miracle and should be respected as one. A child is a blessing that can't be compared with any other blessing on the face of the earth. God gives us children; however, they are his inheritance.

The word of God states: "And the fruit of the womb is his reward" (Psalm 127:3 KJV). Children are truly a blessing to parents. Each child that is born on this earth has a destiny in God. Children as well as adults have a purpose to fulfill. Parents are to guide their children into discovering their destiny for the glory of God. It is their responsibility to train children in the ways of God. "Train up a child in the way he should go and when he is old, he will depart from it" (Proverbs 22:6 KJV).

In the times we are living in today, parents need discernment. It will help to guide their children with a sense of hope, wisdom, and good understanding. God knows children before they are born, and they are very special to God. He desires for them to have a good quality of life.

Children are helpless, and parents are to bring up their children in the love and admonition of the Lord. The Bible tells parents: "But bring them up in the nurture and admonition of the Lord" (Ephesians 6:4 KJV). Parents are to love their children with the love of the Lord. They are innocent and have so much to give. Children need a stable, safe, and secure home filled with love and peace, and without a fearful environment.

Protecting the self-esteem of children is very important. Therefore, a good place to start is to guard the interaction of parents with their children. It is easy to get out of control and not recognize how negative behaviors and attitudes can affect them. Parents' negative interactions with children can become a normal pattern of behavior. Elevating the voice to hollering and screaming isn't a very good pattern to use in training children. Negative interaction patterns could affect the emotional growth of children. Watch out for some of the warning signs!

Depression
Lack of desire to attend school
Withdraws from the family
Low self-esteem

**Parent Alert**

A child is a blessing that can't be compared to any other blessing on the face of the earth.

# God's Gift to Parents

This nation must rise up and again focus on the family, especially the children. Children are God's gift to parents and the world. However, do you think of your children as a gift? Today, bullying is a major societal issue involving children. Bullying can occur in many ways by their peers, teachers, coaches, neighbors, recreational leaders, and even parents.

One of the main types of bullying is the name-calling. Children can be influenced by other children to become lesbian or gay through name-calling. It is very important for parents to talk to children about this subject. Parents can also bully their children. This can leave mental scars that can result in depression, as well as set the child up to have difficulty sustaining good relationships.

Many children attend nursery by the time they are two months old. Sometimes parent training is considered a part of the day-care training. However, training children is the responsibility of the parents. When children start school, parenting isn't a part of the teachers' and administration's job description. Their job is to educate children.

Ask yourself these questions. How often am I spending one-on-one quality time with my children? Do I guide and train my children with rules and consequences? Do I expect the daycare or babysitter to train my children? What responsibilities do I take with the overall training and development of my children? Am I a responsible parent? I believe that parenting children should be a priority in the family.

Parents, open up your heart and your spirit. Parenting is serious business. No child should be left behind due to inadequate parenting. It's not enough to dress up children, give them lunch money, and send them to school. What about the emotional state of children? Are they hurt, wounded, or suffering from a broken heart? Don't let a stranger grow up in your house. Do something with your child every day, to let him or her know you care.

Children want to see parents involved in what concerns them. An example is the PTA.

This is one way you can show an interest in your child. Carpooling is great; however, sometimes children want their parents to attend their activities with them. I believe this is an area in which parents can be a little more sensitive to the spirit of their children. They don't always show their true feelings. Listen to the heartbeat of your children!

**Parent Alert**

Parenting is serious business. No child should be left behind due to inadequate parenting.

## Mistaken Identity

America, we have a crisis in this nation. Children are making decisions to change their gender. Parents are allowing their young children to make their own determination as to who they want to be. They are deciding whether they want to be a girl or a boy. God created male and female, and he is the creator of the universe.

> So God created man in his own image, in the image of God created he him;
> male and female created he them.
> (Genesis 1:27 KJV)

When will this nation respect God? We call out to him when we are in need and experience hurts and disappointments. We even go to church sometimes. Occasionally we wipe off our Bibles and read a scripture or two.

Children need loving parents to instruct them and give them godly guidance. They are not of age to make any kind of major decisions regarding their lives. It is certain that a child shouldn't be given the freedom to change his or her entire identity. He or she is absolutely clueless concerning what his or her life will look and feel like after a dramatic change like this. Parents, please know that you will be accountable to God and man for the actions of your children. You are the adult and the parent. They are the children.

Today, we live the way we want to live. America doesn't acknowledge God. If it feels good, we do it without a conscious. When will the people on this earth wake up? God has truly blessed this nation. He loves all of the children, and he wants their parents to love and protect them. What children need is unconditional love and acceptance—caring and nurturing parents to guide, instruct, and support them.

Parents, monitor your children very closely. Let them feel your love. Help them to grow up into healthy men and women. Children need to have healthy minds, bodies, and spirits as well. They should feel blessed as God has created them. God speaks to the mistaken identity issue.

> For this cause God gave them up unto vile affections: for even their women
> did change the natural use into that which is against nature:
>
> And likewise also the men, leaving the natural use of the woman, burned in
> their lust one toward another; men with men working that which is unseemly,
> and receiving in themselves that recompence of their error which was meet.
>
> And even as they did not like to retain God in their knowledge, God gave
> them over to a reprobate mind, to do those things which are not convenient;
> (Romans 1:26–28 KJV)

# Enough Is Enough!

What is wrong in this nation? We are the United States of America. Our pledge says that we are under God. This means that we are under his authority. The Bible is God's authority in the earth. The currency in our country says, "IN GOD WE TRUST." Is the United States dishonoring God? Could this be the reason we experience so much devastation in this nation and in the family? There is so much corruption in this land. America, stop talking and do something!

We claim to be a thriving country. People come from all over the world to America. We have a reputation of a place where dreams can come true. Many people see us as such a great, successful, and prosperous nation. Look what is happening at our borders. This is evident of what people think of America. And yet this great nation is experiencing poverty and homelessness.

Today, we still have an abundance of homeless people. Many people don't have sufficient clothing, and they go hungry every day. There is so much waste in this country. "A total of 552,830 people were experiencing homelessness on a single night in 2018. This number represents 17 out of every 10,000 people in the United States."[1]

Parents are killing children, children are killing their parents, and children are killing children. Children are abandoned, rejected, abused, and neglected. Children aren't dreaming; they are trying to survive. There are children who don't ever receive love or praise from their parents. When children can't find love at home, they seek it in all the wrong places.

Children look for role models outside the home and find none. They can't respect the CEOs, the government leaders, businessmen, teachers, coaches, administrators, professional sport leaders, physicians, recreation leaders, or community leaders anymore. They have seen so much crime and deceptiveness. Where are the role models for the children? Why aren't the parents assuming their role and responsibility to be their children's role models? Is this too much to ask, or is it that parents don't want to be accountable for the way they think and act?

Let's talk about the children. Are your children happy? Are all of their needs taken care of on a daily basis? When is the last time you took the time to really listen to your child? When is the last time you visited your child's school without an invitation? Do you provide a safe and loving home for your children? Do your children feel loved? Please think seriously about these questions.

Families make up this nation. If they don't have time to train their young and nurture them, who will? There isn't a day care or a nanny in this world that can take the place of a parent's love. Why do we fall into the trap of allowing others to train our children? Grandmothers, other family members, and babysitters are raising the children. However, when something goes wrong with the children, we blame others. Stop it! Can you at least accept your own mistakes? There are some parents who are present in the lives of their children but fail to parent them.

It's time for a change, but first change must happen within. We can't continue to blame others for our parenting failures. Look inside yourself, and make sure you are the parent you desire in your heart to be. If you need to improve, make every effort to find the resources to change. Don't put it off another day. Don't stand in the way of your child's success. Make time in your day for your children.

Don't make excuses! We can find the time to accomplish anything we desire. Wake up before it's too late! Yes, children are going astray. God has given us the power to help shape the destiny of our children's lives. It's not too late. Parents, you can make a difference in reshaping America. Let your children feel your love. Pastor Milford spoke to his congregation: "We have tried to express our love for our children with 'things' instead of spending time with them and teaching our children to work and save."[2]

**Parent Alert**

Families make up this nation. If they don't have time to train their young and nurture them, who will?

"Let My Children Go!"

Stains on my children, where did they come from?
Children filled with pain, wounded, and a grieving heart too.
Let my children go!
Parents want to know why their children are hurting. I did
Everything I could.
Don't tell a lie. You do know why.
Honesty will set you free.
Let my children go!
Stop the lame game; truth is the key,
Set your child free.
Why can't we speak the truth in love?
God knows all of our guilt and our games.
He stands ready to pardon us from the shame.
It's time to make a change.
Let my children go!

—Catherine Smith Robinson

# Notes

1. 2018 AHAR Report: Part I - PIT Estimates of Homelessness in the U. S., December, 2018. https://hudexchange.info

2. Josh McDowell and Bob Hostetler, *Right from Wrong: What You Need to Know to Help Youth Make Right Choices* (Word Publishing, 1994), 49.

# CHAPTER 2

# A House Is Not a Home

Where are the children? They aren't running and playing in the yard. What do you see in their eyes or their faces? When is the last time you saw your child smile and full of joy? Parents, do you have a clue what your child is feeling? Does anybody understand what's happening to the children?

## A War Zone

The children are in a war zone. They want genuine love from their parents. Some parents are too judgmental. Acceptance is what children are looking for. Many are hurting and need to be healed. How much longer will this war go on? There is so much pain! Some children have mixed emotions about how their parents really feel about them. They don't know if their parents care. How many more battles will children have to fight before they win the war? The war of true acceptance!

Parents, children are in a real war. We must save a generation from destruction. Where is the war zone? It starts in the home—the war of not having loving and caring parents that will love them unconditionally. Should parents love their children unconditionally? Do children feel like they are a priority in the eyes of their parents? "We cannot assume that children will know what our priorities are: we must live our priorities. Many a child for whom the parents feel unconditional love receives the message that this love is very conditional indeed."[3] Ask yourself this question and be truthful about your answer. Are the children growing up in a house or a home?

Please check the items that pertain to your dwelling place:
Does your child live in a house or a home?

____A house without love

____A house of unforgiveness and bitterness

____A drug house

____A house with irresponsible parents

____A peaceable house

____A domestic violence house

__A house of rejection

____A house of abuse

____A godly home

____A house of condemnation and guilt

____A house of accusations

____A house of crimes

____A caring home

____A house of prostitution

____A perverted house

____A house of incest

____A stable home

____A house of threats

____A profane house

____A home of unconditional love

____An alcoholic house

____A nurturing home

____A medical drugs addiction house

____A house of rules without role models

____A "do as I say" house

____A latchkey house

____A house of fear and terror

____A house of superiority

____A house of inferiority

____A house of blame and shame

____A house of disrespect

____A responsible home

____A house of neglect

____An "I don't care" house

____An authoritative house

Remember, a house is not a home, and your children are the first to know what kind of house they live in. Would you be afraid to allow your child to complete a questionnaire, in reference to them living in a house or a home? If you are, then you have some work to do.

If every parent reaches out and loves his or her own children from the heart, then a generation can be delivered and set free. If parents don't esteem their children and give them confidence, then who will? It is the parent's responsibility to validate his or her own children. The war in our homes must end. Until parents say yes to ending it, the war continues.

**Parent Alert**

Where is the war zone? It starts in the home-the war of not having loving and caring parents that will love them unconditionally.

## At Risk Sitters

Older children are expected to take care of younger children when parents are away. They are placed in this situation with little or no training. Therefore, many of them are not in a position to take care of their younger siblings. In these kinds of circumstances, they can bully their siblings and be very cruel. Parents must take into consideration that they may be preoccupied with talking on the phone, using the computer, or playing video games. Consequently, the younger children won't receive the proper care. Take another look at the teen sitter! Are your children at risk?

Children are not going to act like adults because they are not adults. Therefore, parents must consider this when requiring them to perform parenting duties. Each state has laws governing older children taking care of younger children. For the safety of the children, parents need to familiarize themselves with their local laws. Prevention is the key to avoiding ignorance of the laws. Good parenting means taking the time to learn what a parent can and can't do. Know your children and what they can handle according to their level of maturity.

Whatever decision parents make in regards to allowing children to take care of younger children, remember that children live what they learn. Whatever they see parents do, they will do. Parents need to be mindful of the kind of role model you are in front of your children. Children will need instructions on boundaries and consequences. Then they will have a sense of what is expected of them.

**Parent Alert**

Children grow up to be healthy adults when they have been granted the right to be children.

# Who's Winning the War?

With children's risky behaviors on the rise, it is certain children and youths are not winning the war. Many of their minds and emotions are locked up in pain. They are making bad choices and decisions, such as taking drugs, dropping out of school, having babies out of wedlock, selling drugs, joining gangs, committing violent crimes, prostituting, killing other people, and committing suicide.

Children are running away from home, becoming homeless, and finding themselves involved in sexual trafficking. Today, this is an open door for pimps who use young girls to sell their bodies as prostitutes. As a result, some young girls end up with sexually transmitted diseases and unwanted pregnancies.

# Gangs

There is a war going on to destroy the lives of the children. The gangs want the children. They promise them a family and love. And yet they teach them to kill, hurt people, and commit violent crimes to get into the gangs. Then they have to be willing to kill and commit other criminal acts to stay in the gangs. The gangs take the anger of the children and train them to hate. They have to give up their minds and emotions to the gang leaders. They no longer can think for themselves. In short, they don't have a life. It belongs to the gang.

# Drugs

When a child learns to smoke, he or she opens up the door to smoking drugs. Smoking nicotine can lead to smoking illegal drugs. Smoking is an individual choice; however, it can result from peer pressure. Most children realize that drugs can kill you. They wouldn't accept someone giving them poison. Peer pressure isn't the real reason children are using drugs. Why are they using drugs?

Many children are looking for painkillers. They want something to make the pain go away. They are willing to try anything. If it makes them high, and they can't feel any pain, they will try it. Children are not usually forced to take drugs. However, there may be some situations where children could be a part of these kinds of circumstances. On the other hand, I think children use drugs due to some inner hurts or feelings. Children use drugs to mask issues they can't solve.

**Parent Alert**

Many children are looking for painkillers. They want something to make the pain go away.

# Teen Pregnancy

Teen pregnancy is often not the choice of the participants of intimacy. Most of the time, it is just a decision to have sex. Unfortunately for the young people, it is sometimes referred to as "having a good time." Sometimes children are ignorant of the consequences of their own actions. Therefore, it is the responsibility of the parent to make sure that children are taught about sex.

Sex education is still very controversial, and parents must not be shy about teaching their children about sex. We should not allow our children to be educated on sex by the books, TV, videos, magazines, or the computer as a main source of information. A wise parent will teach and educate his or her children on sex. Children need to have a good understanding of their sexual development from their parents.

Ignorance can have a high price, when children lack knowledge of sex and its consequences. Too many children are being born into a world of neglect, rejection, and abuse. The key to good parenting skills is unconditional love, good communication, and spiritual guidance with the children.

**Parent Alert**

The keys to good parenting skills are unconditional love, good communication, and spiritual guidance with the children.

# Date Rape

This is an area where young people definitely need to receive specific information on rape. Rape is forced sex. It is sex taking place where one of the persons isn't a willing participant—normally it's the female. Even if they know each other, it is rape. Young people should report rape to the nearest police department. However, in some cases, fear might keep them from reporting. They could fear that parents may find out. It is especially important to report due to an unwanted pregnancy or a disease.

# Smoking

Smoking is an addiction to nicotine and is harmful to the health of children. It is the gateway to taking drugs. Cigarettes are a health risk. Smoking can cause lung cancer, heart attacks, strokes, respiratory and other health issues. "If smoking continues at the current rate among youth in this country, 5.6 million of today's Americans younger than 18, will die early from a smoking-related illness."[4] Secondhand smoking is also harmful, especially to infants and children. However, many parents, due to their addiction, continue to smoke in the presence of their children. It appears that some parents aren't sensitive to the welfare of their children. Parents should never do anything that could jeopardize the health of their children.

# A Tug of War

The school is an institute of learning. It's not a babysitting service, and it's not a training center for students who don't have home training. There are issues between students, parents, teachers, and administrators. Home training is an important factor. However, this is a huge problem with no solution in sight. Some parents seem to be very comfortable leaving a lot of home training to the school. This isn't fair to the teachers or the administration. In order for teachers to teach, they must have good classroom management skills. The students have to be orderly and willing to follow the directions of the teacher.

However, students that exhibit negative behaviors have to be disciplined. It is very unfortunate that some parents make a big fuss when this happens but don't feel the responsibility of making sure their children are properly trained and disciplined. When are parents going to step up to the plate and make a home run for their children? It is very exhausting for teachers to have the responsibility to teach children the curriculum and train them at the same time. A lot of time is lost on a daily basis due to discipline problems. There's definitely a war going on in the schools.

**Parent Alert**

There are issues between students, parents, teachers, and administrators. Home training is an important factor.

# Home Alone

Children don't understand why mother is always busy, and dad is asleep on the couch. When they want to talk, there is no one to talk to. When they finally do get an opportunity to talk to their parents, sometimes they sense that parents don't have time for them. Children need to have quality time to talk to their parents on a daily basis. They can feel alone even when parents are at home if the lines of communication are closed. Parents, recognize when your child needs your undivided attention. Children love their parents and look forward to their attention when they are home.

The way some parents treat their children, it sends them into the streets looking for love. They start to look for love in all the wrong places when they begin to feel neglected and rejected. Yes, you are buying them clothes, and, yes, you are buying them food. This isn't what makes a parent a good parent.

Do you feel that you are really bonding with your children? Children want their parents to feel that they are special. When this doesn't happen, they start to hurt inside. If they have parents that don't communicate with them on an ongoing basis, they can begin to display negative behaviors at school and with other people. One of these is anger. If anger is not controlled, it will begin to get out of control. Parents, listen to the inner voice in the children and protect them from the angry giant on the loose.

When young children are left alone, they are not responsible for their actions. Parents that place their children in this position have left them in an adult role and are totally responsible for what the child does when they are away. We can hardly keep up with the actions of children when parents are at home; therefore, it is impossible to know what they will or will not do when parents are not present.

**Parent Alert**

Children need to have quality time to talk to their parents on a daily basis.

Allowing children to stay at home alone can present dangerous situations to the child, siblings, parents, peers, and even the community. Some children begin to see themselves in a powerful role with absolutely no one to answer to. On the other hand, other children are fearful when left at home by themselves. In time of crisis such as a home invasion, the child must make quick decisions for his or her safety. If the child is alone at home after school daily, is he or she trained on rules for an emergency?

Why are children left alone so much? Parents are to make sure that their children are safe and their needs are taken care of. Do the children feel comfortable alone? Are they comfortable making mature decisions in the face of a crisis? Are they immature and won't be able to make good choices in an emergency situation. Good parenting requires that these kinds of questions are asked, realizing that danger is always a possibility.

It is important that parents know how their children feel about being alone. Do they express any fear about being home alone? Can they be trusted to follow rules? Is there an emergency plan available? Are there any alternatives to staying at home alone? Think about it! If children don't feel safe at home alone, they shouldn't be by themselves.

**Parent Alert**

It is important that parents know how their children feel about being alone.

# Latchkey Children

Latchkey children experience many different kinds of situations. Sometimes they become emotional and fearful, or anger can occur. There are young children that come home from school to an empty house every day. Some are fearful and will tell their parents. Others are fearful and don't tell them. Fear can eventually lead to anger or hurt, when children feel they aren't protected or safe. It is the parents' responsibility to know if their children are experiencing fear. Are your children experiencing latchkey fears?

Parental obligations shouldn't be placed before the safety of children. No parents want to feel that their children are unsafe, fearful, or unprotected. There are always alternate plans parents can make. All children should feel safe. Latchkey children are all colors, sizes, and ages. They are as young as prekindergarten. Some stay home alone, and others stay with siblings or friends. Some children feel safe, and others are fearful and unprotected. Remember, "an ounce of prevention is better than a pound of cure."

**Parent Alert**

Fear can eventually lead to anger or hurt, when children feel they aren't protected or safe.

# Latchkey Preparation

### The Trust Factor

Can you trust your child to follow your directions?
Is your child obedient?
Will your child go straight home?
Will he bring other children into his home?

### Child's Feeling Factor

Is the child afraid?
Is the child apprehensive about being alone?
Talk to the child about anything that worries him or her or makes him or her uncomfortable.

### Safety Factor

Is the home secure?
Does the child know how to work the lock system and the alarm system?
Does the child understand the rules for preparing his or her snacks or meals?
Are there special rules if the child panics or becomes very fearful when he or she comes home?
Discuss cleaning products, medicine, tools, and other equipment in the home.

# Latchkey Basic Rules

1. Make sure that the child has a list of posted emergency numbers including parents by the phone.
2. Give children specific rules for opening the door and answering the phone.
3. Make sure the children know their address.
4. Children should know the family policy about going outside.
5. Make sure children have an emergency kit with a flashlight with batteries.
6. Children should know the escape exit plan in case of a fire.
7. Children should have a neighbor's contact information if needed.

**Parent Alert**

Can you trust your child to follow your directions?

# Notes

3. Gordon Newfield, PhD, and Gabor Mate, MD, *Hold on to Your Kids* (Ballantine Books, 2004, 2005), 196.

4. US Department and Human Services, "The Health Consequences of Smoking—50 Years of Progress: A Report of the Surgeon General," Atlanta, Department of Health and Human Services, Centers for Disease Control and Prevention, National Center for Chronic Disease Prevention and Health Promotion, Office on Smoking and Health, 2014 (accessed Jun 15, 2017).

# CHAPTER 3

# Judge Yourself

Parenting is taken for granted at times with no real concentration on how to raise our children. We can get into a routine of doing things and not focusing on the right and wrong way of doing them. The cares and the frustrations of life can take us to places we don't want to go. They can make us commit acts we never thought possible for us to do. How are you parenting your children? Do you feel that you are doing the best that you can? Take a good look at how you are parenting your children.

What if your child resembles his or her deadbeat dad? Did you try to have an abortion and it didn't work? Is your grandmother raising your children, because you chose a lifestyle of drugs? Is a job or career taking first place in your life? Are you dealing with a negative childhood that affects the way you raise your children? Are you a parent who bullies your children? Our children deserve the best you can give them, no matter what situation you find yourself in. There is always a solution, if you are willing to make sacrifices. Love doesn't cost anything. As adults we know how we want our children to treat us. Can parents also respect their children? Should you demand it and don't give it?

> **Parent Alert**
>
> We can get into a routine of doing things and not focusing on the right and wrong ways of doing them.

## Don't Bully Me!

What is bullying? Bullying is aggressive, consistent negative behavior toward an individual or group of people. Sometimes children are bullied by their own parents. Do you bully your children? Do you bully your mate in front of your children? Children develop hurt and anger from witnessing unpleasant situations with their parents. Most of the time children don't know how to handle this. Many times, they become very angry. This anger can manifest itself in many ways, and it can be in the form of bullying other children.

This can be a means of releasing the pressure that they feel inside and don't know quite how to resolve their own issues. Therefore, parents should model respectful behaviors in front of their children. Parents should think about the kinds of behavior they model in front of their children. When children see negative behaviors at home, they will model them with their peers at school and in the community.

Parents, wake up and understand that children will do what they see, and not as they are told. This is a generation that wants answers. They want to know why this is being done, and why this isn't being done. Even if they don't say it to their parents, they may eventually share their concerns with someone else.

When children bully, they need counseling. They need help in being able to evaluate their feelings. At times, children don't allow themselves to feel pain anymore. They can take out their feelings on others. If the pain is unbearable, the children will probably exhibit anger or reaching out to hurt others. At times they may want to see others hurt because they hurt. When others hurt, they get a sense of gratification. Also, some children can feel empowered when they are able to bully their peers.

Children can become numb to the pain they are causing other children. They begin to like the status they gain with other children, being looked upon as a bully. They enjoy children being afraid of them. Bullies, children that are bullied, and bystanders all need help through the school, parents, and the community. Children want to be safe and secure at school and at home. If children see their parents bullying each other, then the parents are telling their children that it's okay to bully. In the meantime, what are we going to do to stop the bullying?

**Parent Alert**

When children see negative behavior at home, they will model this with their peers at school and in the community.

"Bullying occurs once every seven minutes."[5] It is an unhealthy act. It causes pain and suffering and can be a silent killer. Children have been known to commit suicide. Too many children are victims of bullying. Parents, what kind of sacrifices and commitments are you willing to make? This is an urgent alert call to all parents. The life you save may be your child's. Don't bully your children. Bullying must stop!

"No More Bullying"

You made me cry inside. Your name was Bully.
You came to me when I was a boy.
You came to me when I was a girl.
But I didn't know you. The door was opened, and you came in.
I didn't know how to shut you out.
You were the pain that I felt, but I didn't know why.
No more bullying. Set me free!
I cried and nobody heard my cry.
My heart was torn apart. Does anybody care about me?
The pain was so bad I wanted to die.
I didn't understand why this was happening to me.
Bully, you made me your slave, and I couldn't get free.
The wounds went deep into my soul and pierced me on the inside.
No more bullying. Set me free!
Then I met fear, unforgiveness, bitterness, and anger.
It wasn't long before they took over my life.
Bully, you opened up your arms and welcomed me to stay.
I was in your hands, but I didn't want to stay.
I wanted to run, but you wouldn't let me go.
No more bullying. Set me free!
I cried over and over again, but nobody heard me cry.
I felt my parents didn't care. Did God really care?
He was with me all the time. He never left me.
He restored my soul and gave me the victory.
I am delivered from the enemy of bullying.
No more bullying, I am free!

—Catherine Smith Robinson

**Parent Alert**

The life you save may be your child's. Don't bully your children.

If you continue to do the same things, you will get the same results. I once had a pastor who frequently told the congregation birds of a feather flock together, and they fly to the same destination. What groups are you affiliated with? As parents, we are responsible for our actions and conduct. It is very important to model what we tell our children. Whatever we model, children will more than likely model the same kinds of behavior. We can't expect that we can just live any kind of lifestyle before our children and get the results that most parents desire. Children need the proper guidance each and every day of their lives, and they need good role models.

Communication is one of the keys to good parenting. Taking the time to make sure that you are developing good communication skills with your children is very important. Great caution should be taken in order that children are comfortable talking to their parents. An open-door communication policy with children is a great start. They can communicate with their parents whenever they desire to. If parents don't find the time to talk with their children, they will find someone outside of the home to talk to. The nurturing and bonding of parents and children is of uttermost importance for the success of children.

God gave parents children. God is the creator of children. There is a need to submit ourselves to the word of God to follow godly principles of parenting. The word of God gives us a path as a guide. In order to parent as God would have us to, parents can ask for wisdom (James 1:5 KJV). Wisdom is free to those that ask. But asking must be in faith in order to receive.

**Parent Alert**

The nurturing and bonding of parents and children is of uttermost importance for the success of children.

Parents must judge themselves so they will not have to be judged. When you judge yourself, you can see clearly how you parent your children. If parents look inside of their hearts with a magnifying glass and a spirit of honesty, they will find the areas they need to work on. Honesty and a pure heart will be a blessing to all parents on the journey to parenting.

New parenting skills will be needed during the development of children. Parents shouldn't be in shame or in denial during this process. It is God's will that you walk in the truth and not in error (3 John 1:4 KJV). That means reading the word of God and searching the scriptures to gain knowledge and understanding. In the scriptures are answers to all problems, issues, frustrations, discouragements, hurts, distresses, discontent, disappointments, pain, and sorrow. Repentance is one consideration when parents move closer to the desire to learn more in reference to parenting. Parents can repent to God for themselves and to their children. God will cause a refreshing to come after repentance (Acts 3:19 KJV).

Parents can reach out to God. If you believe that you don't have any sin, then you're not operating in the truth (1 John 1:8 KJV). You basically believe that you don't need God. In other words, "I will do what I want to do. My life is my own to live as I please. However, when trouble or sickness comes, then I will seek God." It is important to seek the face of God and not his hand. When you come to God, you must have a repenting heart and walk in the truth concerning the issues in your life. God isn't a sugar daddy to be used only as needed. The repentance process is necessary to put you in right standing with God. Your confession of sin cleanses you from all unrighteousness (1 John 1:9 KJV).

**Parent Alert**

When you judge yourself, you can see clearly how you parent your children.

# Watch Your Words!

The word of God states that blessings and curses should not come out of the same fountain (James 3:10 KJV). Words have a lot of power. They can bless, or they can curse. The words that are released from our mouths must not be done without thinking. We should think before we express our thoughts. Once we speak, words can't be taken back. The old saying that words don't hurt isn't exactly the truth.

> Death and life are in the power of the tongue: and they that love it shall eat
> the fruit thereof.
> (Proverbs 18:21 KJV)

Words do hurt and sometimes can change a person's destination. Our words should be kind and not hurtful or harmful to others. We shouldn't criticize or embarrass children. It is very important to choose our words carefully. We don't want to offend or persecute them. Negative words can literally destroy a child's life. Children don't always tell their parents when words hurt them. Many times children are silent in regard to the way they feel when parents speak to them.

The silence can become a spirit of unforgiveness, withdrawal, rejection, or anger. Later on, the manifestations of feelings may be acted out in the form of risky behaviors. I've seen and talked to many children with respect to how parents talk to them. Children have many concerns, but in my experience it seems as if parents aren't taking the time to really talk to their children. Many times they are talking at them and not to them. Working as an educator and minister for many years I realized that what parents say to children can truly cause them life or death. Children can feel that life is worth living or it's not.

**Parent Alert**

Once we speak, words can't be taken back. The old saying that words don't hurt isn't exactly the truth.

Words can put children on a path to life or destruction. Will you choose life for your child? Watch your words!

> A wholesome tongue is a tree of life: but perverseness therein is a breach in the spirit.
> (Proverbs 15:4 KJV)

There is a great need for parents to examine what they are saying to their children. The words spoken should be fruitful. Words should edify, and they should build your children up and not tear them down. There is never a reason to use an unclean tongue when talking to your children. Speaking negative words and profanity isn't optional. These words are unfruitful and will break your children's spirit. The use of this type of language could eventually cause children to be wounded and could lead to negative conduct and lower grades in school. It is up to the parent to ask the Lord for guidance in exercising control over his or her tongue. Sometimes this isn't easy, and it is a process.

When we speak in the flesh, it will lead to destruction. But if we speak in the spirit, there is peace and harmony. Watching the words that are spoken to children requires great concentration. We can't always express what we feel. Keep an open spirit to correct and reprove yourself when needed. When parents are angry, it is wise not to talk with their children until they are calm. If you talk while angry, you might say something you didn't mean. Elevating your voice may send signals to your children that you don't like them. It can be harmful or fearful to them.

> A soft answer turneth away wrath: but grievous words stir up anger.
> (Proverbs 15:1 KJV)

Parent, be watchful over the tone you use with your children. We can program our voice so that we don't project anger, even if we are angry. If for some reason we elevate our voices in an angry manner, there is redemption in forgiveness. It is good for children to understand that parents are not perfect, and from time to time they also need to be forgiven. Parents, be mindful that teens are going through hormonal changes and need a more careful tone during communications. Be careful not to provoke anger due to the words or the tone that is used. When the softer tone is practiced, there will be a different response from the children. Please don't use the voice of condemnation, but rather "I want to talk with you."

Don't talk at your children!

Parents, don't let your tongue become the voice of the enemy to destroy your children. Be aware of Satan's devices (2 Corinthians 2:11 KJV). You should bless your children and not curse them. God doesn't want you to praise him with your mouth and then speak evil and unkind words to your children. This is totally unacceptable to God. Parents must try to heed the danger signs when speaking with their children.

> Hear, for I will speak of excellent things; and the opening of my lips shall be right things.
>
> For my mouth shall speak truth; and wickedness is an abomination to my lips.
>
> All the words of my mouth are in righteousness; there is nothing froward or perverse in them.
> (Proverbs 8:6–8 KJV)

Speak the truth in love at all times. We crucify the flesh by walking in the word of God and become victorious in our speaking. This is a process of self-denial. You want to please God rather than man. Understand that he hears your every conversation. As you become more aware that God is omnipotent and omnipresent, you are more careful what you are communicating to your children. Children model what you do and say. God wants parents' words to be a blessing to their children.

Parents, never lie to your children. If you do this, you will develop an unhealthy relationship with your children. Don't make promises you can't keep. If you fail to keep a promise and your intentions were good, admit it and give them the proper explanation. Children have a forgiving heart. Usually children can understand when you take the time to communicate to them. "You can't expect your child to be responsible if you don't keep your word."[6] Children's first encounter with trust is with their parents. If you fail to model good character, how can you teach it to them?

# Watch Your Words Scripture Study Guide

Book of Proverbs

Proverbs 6:2
Proverbs 6:19
Proverbs 7:5
Proverbs 7:21
Proverbs 16:24
Proverbs 8:6–7
Proverbs 16:30
Proverbs 10:18
Proverbs 17:4
Proverbs 11:13
Proverbs 17:7
Proverbs 12:6
Proverbs 17:20
Proverbs 13:2–3
Proverbs 17:27
Proverbs 13:5
Proverbs 17:28
Proverbs 14:3, 5, 7, 25, 23
Proverbs 18:4
Proverbs 15:1–2
Proverbs 18:6–8
Proverbs 15:4
Proverbs 18:20–21

# A Communication Questionnaire

1. What is the usual tone of voice that is used when speaking with your children?
2. Do I talk to my children or at them?
3. Do I lie to my children and feel that I owe them no explanation?
4. Do I use profane language when talking to my children at any time? If so, when does this occur?
5. Do I condemn or make my children feel guilty?
6. Do I bless and curse my children with the same tongue?
7. Do I talk to my children when I am angry and upset?
8. Do I ask my children for forgiveness when I feel that I did something wrong to them? Do I feel that because I am a parent, I would never ask a child for forgiveness?

9. Is my concentration on building a healthy, godly communication relationship with my children?

10. When your children have issues or concerns, do you always provide healing and restoration?

# Love/Hate Relationship

In a relationship, each person should have a good understanding of the kind of relationship it is. There are lines of authority, rules, and respect that must be acknowledged, if there is to be a healthy relationship. In respect to parents and children, there is a godly foundation established in the word of God. Children are to obey their parents in all things. This is the will of God (Colossians 3:20 KJV). It can't be changed by the rules of men. However, it can be disrespected and disregarded in some parent and children relationships. In reference to children obeying their parents, this is the only commandment with promise. The word states that children should obey their parents so that they may live long on the earth (Ephesians 6:1, 3 KJV).

Parents should be careful to operate only in their God-given authority. Never allow hatred, resentment, or bitterness to develop in your heart toward your child. Children need to be disciplined when they don't follow the rules. Parents should be glad if they have boundaries established. Establishing rules is a part of parenting. It is important that parents be aware that children will become more opinionated as they grow older. Do children have the right to have opinions? Parents have to be careful concerning having perfect children. We were not perfect, and our children won't be perfect. It amazes me to see how parents say ungodly and harmful things to their children, when they make statements they don't like.

Agape love, which is unconditional love, should always be the measurement of the feelings of parents toward children. "Children and teenagers need unconditional love and acceptance today no less than they did 30 or 50 years ago."[7] Children need to feel that they are loved, even when they are disciplined. Parents should take caution when disciplining their children. Never discipline while in a raging posture. This could make children feel they are disliked. It is important that parents realize that their actions may formulate future negative patterns in the minds of children later in life.

Sometimes parents use ungodly language and even violent means in correcting their children. Before you act, you must think. Once you perform an ungodly act on a child because you are out of control, you must understand that you might cause an everlasting wound in the heart of the child. Forgiveness is always available, but it isn't always taken advantage of. Watch your words and your relationship with your children. Words can leave permanent scars and damage that could last a lifetime.

## Take a Look in the Mirror

Parents, don't live double lives before your children. They are watching your behavior every day. When you look in the mirror, you see who you really are. The mirror gives you a clear picture of yourself. Children should know who their parents are. They should not get one picture today and another picture tomorrow. Our children will have difficulty trying to bond with parents of multiple personalities. Children want their parents to have a pleasant face and not one that will change in every situation or circumstance. Parents are human; however, much deep thought, control, and concentration is needed when practicing good parenting.

Parents shouldn't take the posture of overreacting to every situation. Children need to have a sense of security in the way they see their parents handling life in general. Also, they are watching how parents cope with crisis and emergencies. If moral values and standards are taught in the home, then children will become very comfortable and secure with the family's belief system. To the contrary, if children see different belief systems operating in their parents, they will become confused and insecure. It is very important for parents to examine their belief system and to stand on what they believe. Parents should realize that this is a part of the character building of their children.

## Microwave Parenting

What is microwave parenting? It is a shortcut to being a real parent. It is the kind of parenting that allows others to parent on their behalf. Parents who really don't want the responsibility of parenting will find themselves on the road to microwave parenting. They will basically give their parenting over to their children's grandparents, older siblings, friends, schools, neighbors, babysitter, or whomever will take the responsibility. Children can even parent themselves.

The microwave parents don't take the time to bond with their children. Therefore, there is little time, if any, for nurturing and communications. The children's welfare is looked upon as the giving of the necessities of life, education, and, of course, whatever they can afford for their children. Parents feel that they are taking care of their children when they provide food, water, shelter, clothing, education, and what their kids want.

Microwave parents don't want to make sacrifices for them, such as taking the time to nurture, give guidance, communicate, give homework instructions, and spend time with them. Some parents focus only on their children being honor students and on participation in school programs and activities. The academic and social development is their main concern. The emotional and mental development is neglected for the most part.

Strict morals are given but not demonstrated. Some parents talk at their children but not to them. Many children are latchkey kids, or an older sibling is left in charge, frequently with little guidance or instructions. The children are told that the parents will be glad when they are grown. Microwave parenting is a scapegoat to true parenting. Children are in the way. Parents feel that they can't focus on their own goals. They see their children as being too much responsibility. There aren't any alternatives to parenting. Someone has to nurture, love, care for, educate, train, guide, and provide a safe environment for the children. Some children of microwave parents can be very troubled.

Microwave parents are those parents who don't want to parent their children. They are on a fast track to get their children out of school and out of their home. They look for ways to avoid being around their children. The microwave parents overload their children with extracurricular and sport activities in order to avoid spending time with their children.

Some parents appear to be mostly focused on themselves. Children can feel rejected when they don't get enough attention from parents. Some of them find themselves participating in smoking, drugs, gangs, dropping out of school, academic failure, bullying, trafficking, juvenile crime, prostitution, and lesbian and homosexual lifestyles. These children are looking for love. Even if they make it in life, emotional issues can still exit. Most of the time, some of these issues are seen later in life as teens and young adults.

**Parent Alert**

Microwave parenting is a scapegoat to parenting. Children are in the way. Parents feel that they can't focus on their own goals.

# Parenting Self-Examination Question

What kind of parent are you? What kind of home have you established for your children? Please note the atmosphere in your home.

Snagging
Complaining
Abusive
Kind
Peaceful
Addictive
Supportive
Peaceful
Moody
Nurturing
Teaching
Murmuring
Negative
Bad attitude
Emotional
Angry
Non parenting parent
Violent
Rejecting
Pervert
Overprotective
Neglectful
Foul mouth
Bullying
Incest
Authoritative
Non affectionate

# Judge Yourself Questionnaire

1. What kind of lifestyle are you living in front of your children?
2. Is your child a latchkey child? If so, are you comfortable with this decision?
3. Have you set behavioral boundaries and consequences for your children?
4. Do you have good communication skills with your children?
5. Do you practice unconditional love with your children?

6.  Are you praising your child for the good things he/she does, or is your concentration on the negative things?
7.  Are you more committed to your profession or job than to your children?
8.  Do you meet your child's teachers and establish a relationship with them every school year, or do you only attend mandatory conferences?
9.  In meeting your child's educational needs, do you attend PTA meetings frequently?
10. Do you make plans for your children to succeed and evaluate these plans often?

# On a scale from one to ten, list your priorities.

_____
_____
_____
_____
_____
_____
_____
_____
_____
_____

11. What do you think your child would say if he/she was asked this question: Do you think your parents love you?

## The Parenting Spiritual Test

1.  How do you rate yourself as a spiritual parent?
2.  Are you walking upright before your children (born again), acknowledging God in your everyday lifestyle before your children?
3.  Are you teaching the word of God to your children? Do you attend church regularly with your children as a family?
4.  Have you led your children to accept Christ as their personal savior? If not, are you waiting on the church to fulfill this responsibility?
5.  Are you monitoring your child's activities such as the use of the computer, video games, television programs, movies, etc. to make sure that they are not developing ungodly behavior?
6.  Are you giving guidance in the love of God by teaching boundaries and consequences to your children?
7.  Are the methods in which you administer discipline to your children according to the word of God?

8. Are you speaking life or death to your children?
9. Do you practice favoritism with your children?
10. Do you practice name-calling with your children?
11. Are your children respecting you and their home rules and responsibilities?
12. Who is in charge of your home—God or the devil?
13. Is there unforgiveness or strife in your home?
14. As a Christian, do you practice any activity that you know is against the spiritual principles of God?

# Judge Yourself Parenting Principles

Scriptural Principles for Parents

Deuteronomy 6:5–9
Deuteronomy 11:19–21
Psalms 71:1–24
Proverbs 1:8
Proverbs 22:1
Proverbs 22:6
Matthew 15:4
Romans 10:9–10
2 Corinthians 7:10
Galatians 5:16
Philippians 2:3
Ephesians 6:1–3
Ephesians 6:4
1 Thessalonians 5:22
1 Peter 2:2
1 John 2:15–16

Teaching Love Principles

1 John 4:7–8
1 John 4:21
1 Corinthians 13:1–8
Matthew 5:44
Matthew 19:19
Matthew 22:37
Matthew 22:39
Matthew 19:19

Teaching the Power of Words

Psalms 19:14
Proverbs 12:22
Proverbs 15:1–2
Proverbs 15:4
Proverbs 16:24
Proverbs 18:21
Proverbs 21:23
Proverbs 15:1
Proverbs 16:24
Matthew 15:18
Ephesians 4:29
James 3:9–10

Teaching Discipline Principles

Deuteronomy 21:18–21
Proverbs 10:1
Proverbs 13:24
Proverbs 19:18
Proverbs 22:15
Proverbs 23:13–14
Proverbs 29:15
Proverbs 19:18
Proverbs 29:17
Colossian 3:20
1 Timothy 5:4

# Notes

5.  National Education Association (2002–17), "Identify Bullying," retrieved from www. nea.org.
6.  Leonard Sax, MD, PhD, *The Collapse of Parenting* (New York: Basic Books, 2016), 125.
7.  Ibid., 105.

# CHAPTER 4

# Save Our Children

This generation is called "the lost generation" by some people. I call it the generation that is looking for the real and that which is genuine. They are looking for loving, supportive parents. Being successful is not their main conversation. Some are mad and some are even bitter. They want to know if their parents really love them. Will they help plan their future? Yes, some children are lost with no direction in life due to poor parenting. They look for parent instructions and guidance contrary to their actions. When they don't have it, children will focus on their peer relationships.

Do we as a society have any plans to reach out and touch the children? They need parents to talk to them and not at them. Our children are waiting in line for directions. Mothers

and fathers, it begins with you. You must show your children that you love them. They need your gentle communication, guiding hand, wisdom, peace, and understanding. Give them your heart!

The school, church, and the community are considered support groups and resources. They aren't parent substitutes! Children are dreamers. Parents can help their children fulfill their dreams by helping them find needed resources. If your child isn't dreaming or thinking about his or her future, talk to your child. Help him or her to dream. One thing to keep in mind is never to give up on your child. Always be there for him or her no matter what. That child needs you, and don't let him or her fail. Say no to poor parenting!

**Parent Alert**

The school, church, and community are considered support groups and resources. They aren't parent substitutes!

# The High Calling of Parenthood

When two people become parents, God's instruction is to bring up their children in the love and admonition of the Lord. He gives specific instructions on how to discipline them. God knew that parents would need many resources to assist them on this sacrificial journey. The main resource is the Bible. The book of Proverbs is filled with a wealth of knowledge in reference to children, parents, and wisdom. Godly parenting is a glorious path. It is also a light to the community and speaks volumes to the world.

Parenting is one of the main priorities in raising a family. It shouldn't take a back seat to professional careers and other jobs. There are ongoing multiple sacrifices that parents will make in rearing children. Monitoring children's spiritual, physical, mental, emotional, and intellectual development is of great importance. Quality time is one of the special needs that should be built into a parent's busy schedule for the proper training of children. Children should feel loved, accepted, nurtured, and secure. Hopefully, all children are treated with love and gentleness. Harshness and foul language have no place in parenting.

**Parent Alert**

The book of Proverbs is filled with a wealth of knowledge in reference to children, parents, and wisdom.

# Train a Child

Training children is the sole responsibility of the parents. Parents are to provide a loving, caring, nurturing, stable, supportive, and secure home in a good environment. The total care of the needs of the children is necessary for their total development. Parents teach values and rules and set boundaries for their children. If boundaries aren't taught, the parent will fail to give them adequate guidance. The evidence of this may be children who lack self-control. This could present major issues in the lives of the children. On the other hand, self-control can lead to success in many areas of their lives. Parents, take charge of your children!

Parents use many methods of guiding and teaching their children. Some people rely on the same style of parenting by which they were parented. Others use psychological and educational parent training. "Think carefully about the virtues you want your children to possess, and teach them diligently. Inscribe them on your children. That means, among other things, that you yourself must demonstrate the virtues you want your child to develop."[8] God is the creator of life, and it is important that parents follow his instructions as it relates to parenting.

Train up a child in the way he should go: and when he is old, he will not depart
from it.
(Proverbs 22:6 KJV)

It is the will of God that parents bring up their children according to the word of God. Training
children is a journey. It takes lots of patience, and it doesn't just happen overnight. Children
need to be nurtured in the word of God. Trusting in God can be the foundation of their lives.
Teaching them how to pray and have faith can help build their self-esteem. God wants parents
to be guided by his word. If God's path is followed, children will please their parents when
they love the word and have the spirit of the Lord. The children will have the desire to follow
the rules of their parents.

**Parent Alert**

God is the creator of life, and it is important that parents follow his instructions relating
to parenting.

In a world of chaos, God speaks to parents to bring up children in the Lord. He wants children
to be successful on this earth. When children are taught to love God, that will definitely make
a positive difference in their lives. They will learn to love themselves first and then how to
love others. The love of God will give them strength and courage. God gives parents specific
instructions in the training of children.

And these words, which I command thee this day, shall be in thine heart:

And thou shalt teach them diligently unto thy children, and shalt talk of them
when thou sittest in thine house, and when thou walkest by the way, and when
thou liest down, and when thou risest up.

And thou shalt bind them for a sign upon thine hand, and they shall be as
frontlets between thine eyes.

And thou shalt write them upon the posts of thy house, and on thy gates.
(Deuteronomy 6:6–9 KJV)

God has called children with a special mission in life. Every child is an individual, and
should not be compared to his or her siblings or other children. Children are unique with
their own gifts and talents. It can be helpful if parents pray for discernment to understand
their uniqueness. Discernment is an avenue to open up doors for parents to meet the needs of
their children. As a result, a stronger bond between parents and children can be established.

**Parent Alert**

When children are taught to love God, that will definitely make a positive difference in their lives. They will learn to love themselves first and then how to love others.

All children belong to God. God has chosen parents to train children. Parents should be very careful how they treat God's little ones. There is never a reason for children to experience abuse of any kind. Parents modeling good behavior and being fair in all situations is very important to God. Children aren't to be treated unfairly and placed in unhealthy situations. It is the responsibility of parents to keep their children safe. Neglect, rejection, and abuse of children have absolutely no place in parenting.

God is the giver of life. When we honor him as the creator, there will be a desire to please him. He has given instructions in his word on how to train the children. The children are a gift from God. They are precious in his sight. He temporarily places them in the hands of the parents. Children are a joy and not a burden. If you feel burdened and troubled in your spirit about how you parent your children, submit yourself to God in prayer. He will give you a loving spirit to parent your children.

## Don't Preach a Sermon; Be a Sermon

Children love to be trained by their parents, giving them the proper rules, boundaries, and consequences. Most children desire to find their pathway to success. They see their parents as people they can trust and look up to for sound advice and direction. Every day children see the parent's role model either as bad or good behavior. It is important to give children clear directions, making sure there is full understanding. When children have to endure a lot of hollering and yelling, it could lead to emotional stress. When there is a significant amount of scolding and loud talking at children, this could mean that there is very little child training being implemented.

Negative times can be used to teach and instruct children in a positive way. Embrace your child and let him or her know that you are concerned, and you care about him or her. Children seem to do much better when they know their boundaries and when they feel loved. If they are loved, then they will learn to love others. If they aren't given love, they won't be able to give it. Love will make children feel safe and secure.

**Parent Alert**

It is important to give children clear directions, making sure there is full understanding.

Encouragement is important to children. When they know that their parents believe in them, they usually develop good self-esteem. A lack of encouragement can be the result of not having parents that believe in their children. However, it is also important that parents who believe in God will teach them to have faith in God. Their trust in God can help them have more confidence in accomplishing their goals.

Children love to be praised and rewarded. They love to be embraced and told they have done something good. Parents, be careful not to focus on the negative behavior but to give recognition to positive efforts and behaviors. Set the bar in the home for the success of your children. When children succeed, there is a great possibility that their parents believe in them. Parents of children who aren't making good progress may need to reevaluate their parenting skills. Building a healthy relationship with children is an extremely important responsibility of parents. Parents, watch out for those special moments when you can teach your child very important life lessons.

**Parent Alert**

Set the bar in the home for the success of your children.

## Parents Mentoring Children

Our children are seeking answers. They want to know who they are. Our children are not silent. They speak loud and clear by their actions. This is how they communicate to the world, that they are hurting. They feel left out and overlooked. Some experience in their emotions the feeling of being tolerated rather than being loved. If children don't find loving parents at home that will help them build their self-esteem, then they will turn to a substitute for love. Their negative experiences can lead to teen pregnancy, drugs, school failure, rejection, anger, crimes, and violence, to name a few.

Have you talked to your child lately? Let's have a moment of truth. Be truthful to yourself. Are you allowing technology to become a substitute for parenting? Children are preoccupied with cell phones, computers, and video games. Every child should be accepted and loved by his or her parents and others. No child should be rejected. Making your children feel loved and teaching them to love themselves and others is a part of the description of good parenting.

**Parent Alert**

Our children are not silent. They speak loud and clear by their actions. This is how they communicate to the world, that they are hurting.

Mentoring children starts at home. Yes it starts with the mother and father. "Mom, Dad, we have let someone else take charge of our children!"[9] Mentoring doesn't start at the nursery, school, or the church. The responsibility of mentoring begins with the parents. Parents are in the position to become mentors for their own children. Parents need to model what they expect to see in their children. Be what you want your children to become. Work on yourself! Don't feel guilt, shame, or condemnation. Making mistakes is a part of the growth process.

Children look up to their parents for understanding and guidance. They need a listening ear. Parents, make time to hear your children. Don't be harsh or hostile! Provide a healthy environment for your children to grow up. Unless parents are willing to guide and direct their children, they will stand alone with no directions. Giving up on your children is not an option. Help your children dream. Find resources in your community to help with their dreams. You don't have to be rich. Take your children to the library and talk to their teachers. Connect with the youth organizations in your community.

**Parent Alert**

Parents, make time to hear your children. Don't be harsh or hostile! Provide a healthy environment for your children to grow up.

I believe parents recognize the importance of training their children. In training, the parents become mentors. They have to keep an open spirit and communication in accordance to the needs of children. A support system is a necessity. Indeed, it takes a village to raise a child. Children have a responsibility to follow the discipline guidelines as taught by their parents. When children and parents have a good understanding, they share a better relationship. Hopefully, this spiritual proclamation will inspire and enhance parent training and mentoring skills.

## What's Love Got to Do with Children?

Real love is unconditional and never fails. When children are wrong, they need guidance from their parents. Love doesn't remind them every time they get it wrong or make a mistake. It covers their mistakes. In the midst of making wrong decisions, children need to know parents care. They need to feel unconditional love. "Children want nothing more than to feel they have our permission to express who they are at any given moment."[10]

## "A Child's Needs"

I need love; don't hate me.
I need acceptance; don't reject me.
I need parents who care.
Give me instructions.
Teach me to do the right thing.
Just don't tell me to do it.
Your actions speak louder than words, so show me.
Listen to me and give me your undivided attention.
Smile with me when I smile; laugh with me when I laugh, and
Cry with me when I cry.
Put your loving arms around me and make me feel secure.
Don't make me look small.
I want to stand tall.
Help me plan my future, so that I can walk in my destiny.
Encourage me!
Inspire me!
Keep me in your prayers.
Don't walk on me and crush my dreams.
If you see me fall, pick me up.
Accept me for who I am.
Love me for who I am.
This is what a child needs.

—Catherine Smith Robinson

**Parent Alert**

Real love is unconditional and never fails.

Love covers all situations and issues. It shows that parents care. Love has a sound. The sound is of security and protection. It doesn't matter what you are going through. Love doesn't change. A statement of love is one of kindness and not evil. The scripture states:

> Charity suffereth long, and is kind;
> charity envieth not; charity vaunteth
> not itself, is not puffed up,

Doth not behave itself unseemly, seeketh
not her own, is not easily provoked,
thinketh no evil;
(1 Corinthians 13:4-5 KJV)

Real love keeps on giving. It is freely given. Children don't have to earn it. Do you put your children in a position of having to earn your love? Is there a desire for your children to please you all the time? Are you always pointing out their faults? Ask yourself, do I possess unconditional love?

Children need love, and they want it. This is what they are looking for. Stop judging them! Make the home environment one of caring and real affection. Parenting isn't easy! When parents have had negative childhood experiences with their parents, they may need to seek professional counseling. Developing good parenting skills is very important, not only for the child. It is also important that parents feel they can have a positive effect on the total development of their children.

## Parent Proclamation

We proclaim that children are a gift from God. We accept the high calling of parenthood—to bring them up in an unconditional loving atmosphere.
We are committed to love them with the love of the Lord.
The generation gap will not separate us from our children.
We take a stand against them being victims of Satan's devices by parental neglect, rejection, or abuse.
We decree that alcohol, drugs, pornography, teen pregnancy, lawlessness, bullying, gangs, cyberbullying, incest, human trafficking, low self-esteem, abortion, perversion, prostitution, juvenile delinquency, or sexually transmitted diseases will not rob the children of their youth.
We accept full responsibility of training our children; however, we look to family members, teachers, coaches, friends, day-care workers, pastors, Sunday school teachers, youth organization leaders, and others to be our support system.
For the Lord wants us to train our children in the way they should go, and when they are old they will not depart (Proverbs 22:6 KJV).
Parents will not withhold correction from their children.
The rod of correction is a part of training children according to the scriptures (Proverbs 23:13, 22:15 KJV).
We come up against all material things that are used to pacify or substitute for genuine loving, caring, and bonding with the children.
We take our place as respectful, responsible, and caring parents.

As parents, we are concerned about the total development of the children. Their emotional, physical, mental, social, and spiritual development are equally as important as the intellectual development.

Parents are subject to God, and children are subject to the parents.

Therefore, parents will not allow their children to assume their role.

The home will be governed by rules, consequences, and boundaries, held together by the foundation of the word of God.

Parents, put on the whole armor of God (Ephesians 6:11 KJV), so that you may be able to discern the spirits that try to attack your children.

We wrestle not against flesh and blood, but the rulers of darkness and wickedness in high places (Ephesians 6:12 KJV).

We will raise up godly children focused on their destiny.

"Looking unto Jesus the author and finisher of our faith" (Hebrews 12:2 KJV).

Pursue the journey of great parenting and watch the benefits of rearing successful children.

—Catherine Smith Robinson

**Parent Alert**

We proclaim that children are a gift from God. We accept the high calling of parenthood--to bring them up in an unconditional loving atmosphere.

# Notes

8.  Ibid., 137.
9.  Josh McDowell and Bob Hostetler, *Right from Wrong: What You Need to Know to Help Youth Make Right Choices* (Dallas, TX: Word Publishing, 1994), 41.
10. Shefali Tsabary, PhD, *The Awakened Family* (New York: Viking, 2016), 93.

# CHAPTER 5

# Abuse: A Child's Worst Enemy

As an educator, I've read and heard many shocking stories. Statistics state that most child abuse takes place with a parent, family member, or someone close to the family. Children need to be protected by their parents. They are innocent and can't protect themselves. A home should be a place of loving, caring, safety, and a peaceful and a healthy environment in which children can grow up spiritually, intellectually, emotionally, physically, and mentally. Do you have a monster in your house?

**Parent Alert**

Children need to be protected by their parents. They are innocent and can't protect themselves.

Parents, take off the mask. Who's watching your child? Be aware! The monster may be in your house. Many abusive activities take place in the privacy of a child's home. If you see it, don't look the other way. Dial 911. Don't neglect your first responsibility to protect innocent children. They can't protect themselves from these monsters. As much as humanely possible, parents must strive to be the best parents they can be. Go the extra mile to make your child safe and secure.

## Sexual Abuse

I believe that this is one of the worst kinds of abuse. This is a great enemy to your children. Why would anyone want to take the innocence of a child? The person that does this horrible act has to be mentally sick. Many times this person is a father who begins a pattern of child abuse in his own home. Sometimes the mother is ignorant to what is happening, and at times, due to fear, she looks the other way. The child doesn't understand what is going on and follows the lead of the abusive parent.

A father can teach his daughter to play special games with him. The child can be told that this is a secret, and she can't share this with anyone else. As the girl grows older, the father may begin to threaten the child, to make sure that she won't reveal their secrets. The child may feel threatened or fearful. Even though she may experience these emotions, she may think her father is expressing his love for her.

Abused children cry what I call "silent tears." These are the tears that cry for help. No one hears the child crying. They are tears cried in the closet, bathroom, on the pillow, and in the heart. Sometimes children are being abused, and parents don't recognize what the child is going through. There aren't any signs of scars; however, there are changes in the behavior of the child. Sometimes parents misinterpret how the child is acting. Parents, watch for all the red flags.

Pay special attention to all teens and adults who supervise your children. This includes sports, after-school activities, churches, camps, and other youth gatherings. Yes, I said churches. I would caution you not to put 100 percent total trust in any person, no matter his or her position or reputation. Today, parents have to play it safe for their children, starting in their own home. Parents, watch for the red flags. If you see them, do something. Don't be in denial. Protect your children!

**Parent Alert**

Abused children cry what I call "silent tears." These are the tears that cry for help. No one hears the child crying.

## Mental and Emotional Abuse

The emotions of a child can be greatly damaged by any person. An emotional or mental abuser could perhaps be a parent, caretaker, family member, or friend who is very close to the child. However, this kind of abuse probably takes place mostly in the homes with their parents. Although there are no visible scars, there are some warning signs associated with this abuse. "The consequences of child emotional abuse can be devastating and long-lasting, and include: increased risk for a lifelong pattern of depression, estrangement, anxiety, low self-esteem, inappropriate or troubled relationships, or a lack of empathy."[11]

## Prevention Tips for Child Abuse

- Don't take for granted that caregivers or sitters are innocent whether they are family or friends. "While it's appropriate to teach our children about 'stranger danger,' it's important to recognize that most child abuse is perpetrated by someone the child knows—a parent, relative, stepparent, or significant other, or family friend."[12]

- Be careful when allowing your children to sleep in the bed with relatives when you are not present.
- Use caution when children attend pajama parties. Take into consideration if you know the parents well and if there are other siblings, relatives, or friends in the home.
- Limit the time you leave your children at home alone.
- Don't leave your children with new neighbors or new friends.
- Don't leave your children with strangers. Proceed with caution if you don't know the person.
- Be apprehensive about allowing your child to attend unsupervised events.
- Take heed in permitting your children to ride with teen drivers.
- Proceed with caution permitting a male to be the primary caretaker of your child.
- If you see red flags, act immediately. Don't ignore!
- Establish rules with your children. Give them good understanding about relationships and boundaries. Go over them periodically, to see if any of the rules have been violated.
- Keep the doors open for good communication with your children. Then they will be comfortable sharing with you.
- Don't interrogate or probe! If this happens, you might make your child fearful and scared. Be careful that you don't put them in a position to back away from family talks.

# Notes

11. Steven W. Kairys, Charles F. Johnson, Committee on Child Abuse and Neglect, *The Psychological Maltreatment of Children—Technical Report* (2002), Pediatrics 2002109:e68 http://pediatrics.aappublications.org/cgi/content/full/109/4/e68.
12. M. Gary Newman, LMHC, with Patricia Romanowski, *Helping Your Kids Cope with Divorce the Sandcastles Way* (New York: Random House, 1999), 37.

# CHAPTER 6

# A Fatherless Generation

Every child has a birth father; however, giving birth to a child doesn't make you a real father. A father living with his children doesn't make him a father. Some fathers don't work or pay bills. Others may not show love or concern for the welfare of their children. A real father shows love, dedication, and commitment to his children. He is a provider for the needs of his family including support and security.

Fathers are the leaders in their homes, and they take good care of their families. Some fathers are divorcees, separated, or have never married. Many fathers elect not to parent their children and give up their rights to fatherhood. Their children are the victims of a fatherless generation. However, there are fathers who have good reasons for not parenting, due to mental disabilities.

**Parent Alert**

Many fathers elect not to parent their children and give up their rights to fatherhood.

Parents may need to have a clearer understanding of the different kinds of fathers.

## Types of Fathers

### Present/Present Father

This is the birth father that is physically present in the home. He contributes to the physical, mental, social, and intellectual growth of his children. He is a good provider for his children. The father gives directions, guidance, and support. There is a definite relationship between him and his children, and they have an open communication. He is concerned about the total development of his children. This dad is an active father.

## Present /Absent Father

This type of father is physically present in the home. He doesn't participate in the training of his children. He doesn't cultivate a relationship with them. There isn't any father and child bonding. He is a father in name only. He may or may not provide for the financial needs of the children. This dad is very passive. He isn't involved in the welfare of the children. It is as though they don't exist.

## Absent/Present Father

This type of father is absent from the home but present in the concerns, needs, and the total development of his children. He attends the school and community activities of his children. He doesn't allow his position as an absentee father to interfere with the bonding with his children. He focuses on having quality time, open communication, guidance, and support for his children.

## Absent/Absent Father

This type of father is absent from the home and absent from the lives of his children. The father could be a divorcee, separated, widower, never married, or homeless. For these fathers, raising children isn't their priority. Some children may receive many unfulfilled promises, and others may not have the opportunity to talk to their fathers.

The absent father doesn't attend any of his children's school community activities, even the most important ones such as graduation or special school day programs. The children have absolutely no relationship with their father. Some haven't ever seen their father. The father has no concern for the welfare of the children and has made a definite decision to give up all rights to fatherhood.

I have talked to some of my students, and some have said they didn't have a father. I explained to them that they have a father, even if he isn't present in the home. They didn't seem to have a good understanding about the existence of their father. Some of them had never seen their father or communicated with him. And many children have absentee fathers today. For these reasons, I call this generation a "fatherless generation."

Many unmarried fathers give up their right to father their children. They take absolutely no responsibility in contributing to their care and welfare. Therefore, the mother has the burden of taking care of all of the needs of children. Unmarried fathers, make a definite effort to love and support your children. They belong to you, and financial arrangements should be made to take care of them. Treat your children the way you want to be treated.

# Where Are the Fathers?

Where are the fathers? Can you hear the voices of your children? Do you feel their broken spirits? When was your last visit or talk with your children? Do you keep your promises? Are you a good provider? Have you seen the anger in their faces? Are you a real father or have you given up your rights to fatherhood?

Children are crying, and some are emotionally traumatized. They aren't grown; they are only children. As parents, we can't expect them to understand the actions of an absent father. It is hopeful that fathers will feel the responsibility of communicating with their children. How can fathers take the easy road and leave the rough roads for their children to travel without their support? "Sons and daughters growing up with little or no contact with their fathers can be at risk of some damaging effects."[13]

Fathers, where you? Can you hear the cry of your fatherless child? Are you deaf? How can you mistreat an innocent child? They are God's creation, and he gave them a father to take care of them. Do you realize that children are a gift from God? And you have the audacity to throw your gift away. There are people who wished they could have a son or a daughter. All the fathers that walk away from their children and said no to raising them, please repent. God will forgive you.

---

**Parent Alert**

Do you realize that children are a gift from God? And you have the audacity to throw your gift away.

---

Where Is My Father?

I don't know why my father is not here.
Is there something wrong with me?
Did I forget to take the trash out or clean my room?
Maybe it's because I got a C on my report card?
Once my father said he never got a C when he was in school.
Wait, I know! He expected me to be perfect just like him.
"Sorry, Dad I tried, but I guess I missed the mark."
"Where is my father?" said the beautiful little girl.
I've been thinking about my daddy. Where are you?
I cry real tears on my pillow at night. I really want my daddy.
Why didn't you come to parent night, or my first piano recital?
I miss you putting your arms around me, when I'm scared of the dark.

A football player cried out in anger, "Where is my daddy?"
You missed all of my ball games this season. Did you divorce me when you left my mom?
Did I do anything wrong? Why did you leave me?
I'm only a child; I'm not a grown-up.
Why did you stop loving me?
I still love you, Daddy, and I will always love you.
I just really don't understand what happened, and I'm in so much pain.
You didn't say goodbye, and now all I can do is cry.
Where are you, Daddy?
I'm so alone.
I need you, Daddy.
I love you.
Do you love me, Daddy?

—Catherine Smith Robinson

**Parent Alert**

You missed all of my ball games this season. Did you divorce me when you left my mom?

Children love their fathers, and they need them to be an active part of their lives. They look up to them for protection and security. Some children are wounded, growing up without a father in their home. Many are very angry and devastated. Children that experience a lot of anxiety, angry, and hurt in regard to their absentee fathers need to feel free to talk openly with the other parent about their feelings. If there is emotional and negative behavior continuously, counseling may be needed.

## Dad, Don't Divorce Your Children

Every child needs both of his or her parents. It is very important for parents to take the responsibility to parent their children. Single parenting shouldn't exist. If two parents are alive and well, both parents should accept the responsibility to parent their children. One parent shouldn't have to parent alone. There are circumstances when parents are physically separated from their children. However, this isn't a free pass for a parent to neglect his or her duties.

Divorce resembles death in that a relationship between two people as it was once known has expired. The reason for which they were joined together no longer exists. It is the death of a relationship. "It's important to realize that getting over a divorce takes a great deal of time. It requires tremendous personal adjustments for both parents and children."[14] The family structure as it was once known has been destroyed. There are no more family traditions, holiday festivities, or special family events. The journey of parenting in their home together has ended.

One of the main reasons for the separation of children and parents is divorce. Most of the time, divorce is a very sad and unpredictable time for the family, especially the children. When the father leaves, there might not be adequate income for the family to maintain their same living arrangements. This can mean children could be uprooted from their schools, friends, and neighborhoods. With this type of adjustment, negative emotions such as fear and anger might surface.

Parents can be a great source of support by communicating more with their children and allowing them to articulate their true feelings without condemnation. Love and support is critical during this time. Communication between fathers and their children should be a priority in their relationship. Children need to know that parents are listening to them and that their feelings count. Only coward fathers dodge their obligations to maintain a healthy relationship with their children.

**Parent Alert**

Divorce resembles death in that a relationship between two people as it once was known has expired.

## Turning the Hearts of the Fathers to the Children

And he shall turn the heart of the fathers to the children, and the heart of the children to their fathers, lest I come and smite the earth with a curse. (Malachi 4:6 KJV)

Fathers have a God-given responsibility to be leaders in their homes. They are to guide, direct, train, love, teach, provide support and security, and be a good provider. All children need to know that they are loved by their fathers. When they lack their father's love, it can sometimes trigger deep wounds and hurts. Absentee fathers can express their love to their children in many ways, even if they aren't present in their homes. One of the most important things that a father can do is to keep his promises to his children.

Fathers, be responsible for your children. Don't neglect to provide financial and emotional support. Fathers should be concerned about the total development of their children. Tell your children the truth. Be a good role model for them. Don't let anything come between you and your children. Don't let anything separate you from your children. They need their fathers, and you need them. Fathers, don't divorce your children!

---

**Parent Alert**

Fathers, don't divorce your children!

---

Children need their father to validate who they are. Fathers have a special place in the hearts of children. When the father is missing from their lives, there is a missing link in the child's development. Many negative behaviors of children are attributed to the absence of fathers in the home. "Children may endue significant emotional damage if a relationship with that parent is denied or severely limited."[15]

Sons need to see their fathers as real men. They need to experience the love of a caring father, even if he doesn't live in the home. Fathers, please pray and ask God to give you a heart for your children. If you do this with a sincere heart, God will direct you to do the right thing. Your children are waiting!

# The Father's Questionnaire

- Are you a real man?
- What kind of father are you?
- What is your destiny in life?
- Why did you father children?
- Do you take the responsibility of being a father to your children?
- As a divorcee, did you divorce your children?
- Do you feel that your children experience the love of a father?
- Do you spend quality time with your children?
- Do you bully your children?
- Do you set boundaries and consequences with your children?
- Since your divorce, do you believe that your children know that you love them?
- In what ways do you show your children unconditional love?
- Are you a good provider for your children?
- Are you a role model for your children?
- Are you an active participant in your child's life?

# Notes

13. Carl E. Pickhardt, PhD, *The Everything Parent's Guide to Children and Divorce* (Massachusetts: Adam Media, 2006), 215.

14. Craig Everett, PhD, and Sandra Volgy Everett, PhD, *Healthy Divorce* (San Francisco: Jossey-Bass, 1994), 17.

15. Ibid., 113.

# CHAPTER 7

# Family Restoration

The Lord is my shepherd; I shall not want.

He maketh me to lie down in green pastures: he leadeth me beside the still waters.

He restoreth my soul: he leadeth me in the paths of righteousness for his name's sake.
(Psalm 23:1–3 KJV)

Before we can even consider restoration, there must be forgiveness. It is easier said than done. There must be good understanding about what it means to forgive. Forgiveness will stare everyone in the face one day. The decision to forgive will be uniquely yours. No one else can make the decision for someone else to forgive. The will to forgive will affect every part of a person's life. Without a doubt, it will touch the lives of the people closest to them.

## Forgive Our Sins

As parents, the test of times is being able to forgive ourselves, spouses, children, and our family members. Many times we nurse our wounds and allow layers of hurt to form within us. The bigger picture is that we feel unforgiving, bitter, and resentful. We protect ourselves from future hurts through separation and isolation. Then the problem becomes more complicated. "Delay only deepens resentment and makes matters worse. In conflict, time heals nothing; it causes hurts to fester."[16]

A major concern in forgiveness is offense. When we are offended by the behavior of our children, family members, or others, it is to our advantage to quickly address it. If it isn't addressed, it could lead to unforgiveness. According to the scriptures, Christians are to go to the offender directly and resolve an offense. If they are willing to do this, the relationship might be saved and unforgiveness can be avoided. Where there isn't closure, a person can open themselves up to a toxic spirit of unforgiveness. The pain associated with the offense can bring deeper hurts and wounds.

**Parent Alert**

The will to forgive will affect every part of a person's life. Without a doubt, it will touch the lives of the people closest to them.

When forgiveness is released, the pain subsides, and the wound is healed. On the other hand, what if the choice is made not to forgive? As parents, it is up to us to set good standards of behavior for our children. Unforgiveness will delay restoration with our children, family, and others. Forgiveness is a powerful act. It takes courage to forgive. Unforgiveness is a cowardly and selfish act. Our children will model what we do and not necessarily what we tell them. What does Jesus say about forgiveness?

> And when ye stand praying, forgive, if ye have ought against any: that your Father also which is in heaven may forgive you your trespasses.

> But if ye do not forgive, neither will your Father which is in heaven forgive your trespasses.
> (Mark 11:25–26 KJV)

The word of God is very clear on forgiveness. If we want to be forgiven, we must forgive. This applies to our children as well as adults. We Christians must be careful not to accept our ways as God's way. No one likes to be hurt by another person. If a person is offended, it is his responsibility to go to that person with the hope of restoration. This is the will of God. If the offended Christian won't follow God's plan, then he is following his own will. What is Jesus's plan?

> Moreover if thy brother shall trespass against thee, go and tell him his fault between thee and him alone: If he shall hear thee, thou has gained thy brother.

> But if he will not hear thee, then take with thee one or two more, that in the mouth of two or three witnesses every word may be established.

> And if he shall neglect to hear them, tell it unto the church: but if he neglect to hear the church, let him be unto thee as an heathen man and a publican.
> (Matthew 18:15–17 KJV)

The responsibility of a Christian is to obey the word. His word should be the final authority in their lives. Forgiveness is powerful. It can set a person free. When we forgive, we walk in the integrity of God's word. We are protected by him, if we make the commitment to follow his word. As parents, we have to forgive our children 100 percent no matter what they do.

**Parent Alert**

Unforgiveness is a cowardly and selfish act.

Unforgiveness is a destroyer tactic of the enemy. It attempts to rob people of having relationships with their children and others. People are placed in bondage when they make the decision not to forgive. They are causing their own problems and holding themselves hostage. If forgiveness is accepted as a way of life, freedom is gained, and pain can be released. "It doesn't help anyone for you to live in pain. You have the most to give to others through embracing and forgiving yourself."[17] You must forgive others too. Restoration can never happen without the truth of forgiveness.

**Parent Alert**

When we forgive, we walk in the integrity of the word of God.

# Restore Our Children!

Families need to be healed and restored. It is time for parents to take a good look at their relationship with their children. There is so much pain and suffering in the world. When I look through the eyes of an educator, I see so many children in anger. Some children talk openly at school about how they feel; however, most will talk when they are in trouble. Children discussed the pain of divorce, absent fathers, noncommunicating parents, home alone, sibling parenting, lack of necessities, domestic violence, drug parents, bullying parents, and others.

It's time for parents to pay strict attention to the total development of their children. Children love name brand clothes, popular toys, and the latest in technology. Most of them want their parents' unconditional love above everything else. They want to be heard, and they want their parents to talk to them. They need attention and guidance. Quality time is something that children desire and need. How can they get to know their parents without it? Parents, open up your eyes and your spirit. Be honest with yourselves. What is the physical, mental, social, intellectual, and emotional state of your child? Is your child wearing a scar that is invisible? If so, why is it that you haven't noticed it? Is there a cry in his voice? Have you heard it? Why not? Our children need to be healed and restored.

"Restore My Soul!"

When you are in a battle, trust God and call upon his name.
Put on the whole armour of God that you will be able to stand against the wiles of the devil (Ephesians 6:11 KJV).
He is your deliverer and your healer.
He loves you!
He will direct your path.
He is your peace and your comforter.
No matter what you are going through,
Lift your voice in adoration, and give God the highest praise.
God is a shelter in the time of need.
He is our rock, when we are weary.
When we have no place to go, he is our habitation.
Be thankful and glorify the Lord.
Exalt his holy name.
He alone is worthy of all praise.
He will give you an encouraging word.
God will never leave you or forsake you (Hebrews 13:5 KJV).
Can't you feel his presence?
He hears your prayers and comforts you.
He died for you that you might be healed,
Of every wound, hurt, and a broken heart.
He shed his blood on Calvary and now do you see?
He's restored your soul, and you are free.

—Catherine Smith Robinson

**Parent Alert**

What is the physical, mental, social, intellectual, and emotional state of your child?

God wants children to be healed and restored. He wants the same for the parents. Everybody makes wrong decisions and choices from time to time. It is time for parents to take the lead in restoring their families. In order to restore children, parents must recognize their mistakes. "Guilt is a predictable and understandable reaction to the awareness that we have hurt someone we love—especially a child. Admitting to mistakes and making a commitment and a plan for change is crucial to your healing."[18] Parents should strive to have healthy families. Restoration is God's idea.

There is a loud cry coming from the children. It's the season to get in tune with their cry. Too much time has already passed. We must not fail to let them see our unconditional love. The church is empowered by God to bring healing and restoration to the youth through the word of God. Children need to be set free from despair and hopelessness. The Youth Proclamation is to the church recognizing and responding to the cries of the youth.

## Youth Proclamation

We proclaim that children are an heritage of the Lord (Psalms 127:3 KJV).
They are blessed and not cursed.
We decree that our youth are blessed in the city,
and blessed out of the city (Deuteronomy 28:3 KJV).
They are the head and not the tail (Deuteronomy 28:13 KJV).
They are the light of the world (Matthew 5:14 KJV).
Today we take back what Satan has stolen from our youth.
We take back their moral values, self-esteem, and loving relationships.
We bind suicide, low self-esteem, abortion, unworthiness, fear, failure, rejection, abuse, peer pressure, fornication, perversion, prostitution, bullying, alcohol, tobacco, lawlessness, mammon, teen pregnancy, pornography, sexually transmitted diseases, cyberbullying, human trafficking, sexual trafficking, gangs, and drugs that will attempt to destroy the lives of young people.
We loose the power of the spoken word of God to our youth.
They will not fight with weapons, but they will fight with the word of God.
The sword of the Spirit is their God-given weapon (Ephesians 6:17 KJV).
They will not have the desire to destroy human lives.
Parents, teach and train your children with the word of God (Proverbs 22:6 KJV).
Help them to stand against the wiles of the devil (Ephesians 6:11 KJV).
Our youth will no longer try to please man, but they will please God. He is Alpha and Omega—the beginning and the ending (Revelation 1:8 KJV).
We destroy the works of Satan to bring about a perverted society of lesbians and homosexuals (Romans 1:24–28).
God created male and female to be fruitful and multiply (Genesis 1:27-28 KJV).
We come against religious spirits that manifest themselves in the form of cults and atheists who believe that there is no God.
Corrupt minds are being delivered by the power of God.
Evil imaginations, vain thoughts, mental and tormenting spirits are cast down.
A sound mind shall prevail in our youth.
Youth, let the mind of Christ Jesus be in you (Philippians 2:5 KJV).
The Lord has not given you the spirit of fear, but of power, love, and a sound mind (2 Timothy 1:7 KJV).

—Catherine Smith Robinson
Revised 2010

**Parent Alert**

We proclaim that children are an heritage of the Lord (Psalms 127:3). They are blessed and not cursed.

# A Healing Heart

As families, we have experienced some very difficult situations and circumstances. What is the pain that you haven't released? Are there struggles of unforgiveness? Are there deep emotional wounds that grip your heart? Repent! Only God can heal a wounded heart. Put all of your trust in him.

> The spirit of the Lord is upon me, because he has anointed me to preach the gospel to the poor; he hath sent me to heal the brokenhearted, to preach deliverance to the captives, and recovering of sight to the blind, to set at liberty them that are bruised,
> To preach the acceptable year of the Lord
> Luke 4:18 KJV

There is restoration for families and others in your life to be made whole. But you have to be willing to let go of the pain. God loves you and everything that concerns you. His heart is toward those that have a repenting heart. When we cry out to him with a sincere heart to accept his word, he hears us. It is his desire to heal your heart. "Thousands of adults bear deep scars from wounds inflicted on them in childhood. There's a great need for inner healing."[19] Don't wait another day. Let God heal all of your hurts. Your true destiny awaits you!

A Prayer of Deliverance

Out of the depths of my soul I cried, Abba Father. Where were you when I was buried in my own tears? My heart was overwhelmed. Did you not hear my cry?
My body felt like I was in quicksand. I couldn't move! My hands and arms were covered with sweat. I couldn't breathe as I grasped for air. I thought I was going to die. The cry of my heart was like an explosion on the inside of me. I desperately needed to hear from you. I was desperate to hear your voice and to feel your touch. Then I gripped my fists and said that I didn't want to die.
I called out in my grief, sorrow, and pain. How long will I have to bear this in my heart? How long will I have to suffer?
Alpha and Omega, the beginning and the end (Revelation 1:8 KJV), do you hear my cry? Are you listening to me?

O Lord, do you really care?

I want to trust your holy word. You said that you would be with me in the fire. You said that you would be with me in the storm. I feel like I'm drowning in my own tears.

Where are you, Abba Father? You said that you would never leave me nor forsake me.

Fear not; I never left you. I was right by your side. I heard your voice crying in the wilderness. I spoke peace to you, but you didn't hear my voice. I told the waters of your troubles to stand still, but there was no response.

I put my loving arms around you, but you rejected me.

I told the fire not to burn you, and you put your trust in man. You refused to hear my voice. I wanted you to touch my word with your faith, so you could be made whole. But you walked away in fear.

My son, my daughter, I never left you. I heard your voice over and over again. I spoke peace to you, but you didn't respond to me. I told the waters of your pain not to overflow you. And you had not a listening ear. I put my loving arms around you, but I didn't receive your embrace. I heard you pray for the Lord to deliver you and that you couldn't take it anymore.

Why did you have to suffer so long, my child?

It was because the word without faith is unbelief. Healing comes by releasing faith in the word of God. The answer to the cries of your heart is that I never left you. I didn't forsake you. I was there all the time and I'm still here.

—Catherine Smith Robinson

---

**Parent Alert**

Don't wait another day. Let God heal all of your hurts.

---

God wants the best for parents, and he doesn't condemn them for their failures and mistakes. There is no pointing of the finger as the world would have it. God's ways are not like the world. He loves us when we are unlovable. He is always interceding for us. The Lord is our Shepherd, and he gave his life for us. He keeps his promises through his word, and he wants us to be healed from all of our sorrows, disappointments, hurts, and pain. God wants us to yield to him in order to overcome our pain. Be set free from the cries in your heart. Rise up and be healed!

Healing, deliverance, and restoration come from the giver of life—the Lord Jesus Christ. He wants to heal the family and give you a brand new start. He won't condemn you or find fault because he loves you unconditionally. The Lord wants you to accept the sacrifices he made for you at Calvary.

It is my prayer that you will take this opportunity to reach out to Christ today and give him all the glory for all the things he has done. I believe that accepting the Lord Jesus Christ is the path to becoming the great parent you want to be. This prayer will guide you into the exit of your past, into your glorious new future with the Lord.

Salvation Prayer for Parents

Dear God,

I need your help to be a better parent. I thank you for drawing me to you by your spirit. Today, I accept the Lord Jesus Christ into my life. I confess with my mouth and believe in my heart that you died and arose again for my sins. I am eternally grateful for your guidance and direction in teaching me how to love my children unconditionally as you love me.

Thank you for being my Lord and my savior.

The salvation scriptures states:

> That if you shalt confess with thy mouth the Lord Jesus, and shalt believe in thine heart that God hath raised him from the dead, thou shalt be saved.

> For with the heart man believeth unto righteousness; and with the mouth confession is made unto salvation.
> (Romans 10:9–10 KJV)

# Keys to Having a Healthy Family

1. Love and care for each other unconditionally.
2. Learn to communicate effectively (clearly and concisely).
3. Trust in each other.
4. Respect each other.
5. Support each other.
6. Allow for differences of opinion.
7. Spend quality time together.
8. Participation in family decisions.
9. Fulfillment of home responsibilities.
10. Teach family morals and values.
11. Listen to each other.
12. Set family goals.
13. Have regular family meetings.

## Family Proclamation

I decree in the name of Jesus that all members are saved, baptized in the Holy Spirit, and shall fulfill their God-given destiny. The blood of Jesus covers our family because we are in covenant with him.

We are planted in the house of the Lord, and we shall flourish in the courts of our God. We shall bring forth fruit in our old age (Psalms 92:13-14 KJV).

Our family shall walk by faith, and not by sight (2 Corinthians 5:7 KJV). We fear God; therefore, we obey God rather than men (Acts 5:29 KJV). To obey the Lord is better than sacrifice (1 Samuel 15:22 KJV).

The sin that so easily beset us is in our past will no longer have dominion over us.

I bind it in the name of Jesus. We will submit ourselves to God and resist the devil, and he will flee (James 4:7 KJV). We are free from the bondage of sin.

Our family is blessed and not cursed. We are clothed in God's righteousness; therefore, generational curses are bound by the word of God. We are redeemed from the curse of the law (Galatians 3:13 KJV), and the blood of Jesus covers us.

Our children will not be born with physical deformities and mental illnesses. Our children will obey their parents in the Lord. This is the first commandment with promise that they may live long on the earth (Ephesians 6:1–3 KJV).

Mothers and fathers will live godly lives before their children. Parents will teach their children the word and will be godly role models and mentors for their own children.

Our family will walk in unconditional love. We have perfect peace because our minds are stayed on the Lord (Isaiah 26:3 KJV). In all our ways, we acknowledge God, and he will direct our path (Proverbs 3:6 KJV).

I bind sicknesses, diseases, accidents, injuries, or any attacks of the enemy that would attempt to come against us. Jesus died that he might defeat all of the works of the devil. There is no weapon that is formed against us that shall prosper (Isaiah 54:17 KJV). The greater one in us is greater than he that is in the world (1 John 4:4 KJV).

I bind the spirit of hurts and wounded hearts. I loose the healing virtue and peace of God, to bring restoration and healing. By Jesus's stripes we are healed (1 Peter 2:24 KJV).

I bind unforgiving hearts and the spirit of bitterness. Our hearts are clean, and we have the spirit of God. We shall forgive others so that Christ can forgive us.

Thank the Lord for our marriages. I decree that our marriages will glorify the Lord, always abounding in the love of God. The husbands are to love their wives (Ephesians 5:25 KJV). Honor them as the weaker vessels, so their prayers will not be hindered (1 Peter 3:7 KJV).

The wives are to submit themselves to the Lord and to their own husbands (Ephesians 5:22 KJV). Strife will not reign in their homes because it brings forth every evil work.

Praise the Lord for the mind of Christ (1 Corinthians 2:16 KJV). Our mind is blessed.

We cast down imaginations and things that exalteth itself against God's knowledge, and bring into captivity every thought to the obedience of God's word. (2 Corinthians 10:5 KJV).

We will not walk in the lust of the flesh, but we will walk in the spirit (Galatians 5:16 KJV). Lord, we lay at the altar all hindrances that will block the work of the Holy Spirit in our lives. We will endeavor to do all that God has commanded us to do. We give him all the praise and all the glory.

In Jesus' Name. Amen.

—Catherine Smith Robinson
Revised 2019

# Notes

16. Rick Warren, *The Purpose Driven Life* (Michigan: Zondervan, 2002), 155.

17. Joshua Coleman, PhD, *When Parents Hurt* (New York: Harper Collins, 2007), 171.

18. Ibid., 31–32.

19. Zig Ziglar, *Raising Positive Kids* (Tennessee: Oliver-Nelson Books, 1985), 201.

# Appendix A

Parent Resources

Infants-teens, Divorce, and Stepfamilies

Programs
Parenting Books
Parent Involvement
Character Education
Parenting DVDs
Parenting Workshops
Parenting Classes
Parenting Training
Online Learning Center
Spanish Materials

3 CDC-Centers for Disease Control and Prevention www.cdc.gov/ncbddd/childdevelopment/

Child Development

Developmental Screening
Children Mental Health
Free Materials
Positive Parenting Tips

Articles
Research

Multimedia Tools
Early Childhood

www.uen.org/parents/early.php
www.cdeca.gov/sp/cd/re/parentresources.asp

Hearing Loss

www.cdc.gov/ncbdd/hearingloss/parentguides/resources

US Department of Education
www.z.ed.gov/parents

Early Childhood
Special Education
Pay for College
Reading Resources
Help Your Children Learn
Laws and Guidance
Data and Research

US Department of Education
Parents and Families www.ed.gov/parent-and-family-engagement

Programs and Guidance
Staying Healthy
Succeeding in School and Beyond

Office of Special Education www.2.ed.gov/about/offices/list/osers//indep.html

Infants-Age 21

Resources for Special Education including Publications
Archived Publications
Information Products
Health Development
Developmental Milestones
(Birth to Adolescent)
Children's Mental Health
Free Materials
Positive Parenting Tips
(Birth to 17 years of age)

Articles-Scientific Research
Multimedia Tools

Disability Children

www.parentcenterhub.org
www.supportresourcesforparentsidamerica.org/parents

Hearing Loss

www.supportresourcesforparentsidamerica.org/parents

Free Resources

www.discoveryeducation.com/parents
www.jumpstart.com/parents/resources
www.EtiquetteMoms.com
www.teachchildrenesl.com

Children Ministry

www.truthforkids.com
www.wmu.com
www.ichild.co.UK
www.kidsministryresources.com
www.ministry-to-children.com
www.childgrief.org/resources.htm

Drug Free Kids

www.drugfree.org/resources
www.dare.org/keeping-kids-drug-free
www.teenzeen.org/resources.html
www.easyread.drugabuse.gov
www.prevention.org

Magazine

www.Scholastic.com/parents/resourcescollection

Science

www.nsta.org/parents

Parents and Childcare Provider

www.childcareta.acf.hhs.gov/parents-and-providers

Divorce

www.nycourts.gov/divorce/parent_resources.shtml
www.childrenanddivorce.com

# Appendix B

Parenting Skills Evaluation

Name five of your parenting strengths

1. _____

   _____

2. _____

   _____

3. _____

   _____

4. _____

   _____

5. _____

   _____

Name five of your parenting weaknesses

1. _____

   _____

2. _____

   _____

3. _____

4. _____

_____

5. _____

_____

Name ten daily positive parent/child interactions

1. _____

_____

2. _____

_____

3. _____

_____

4. _____

_____

5. _____

_____

6. _____

_____

7. _____

_____

8. _____

_____

9. _____

_____

10. _____

_____

Name ten praises you give your children

1. _____

_____

2. _____

_____

3. _____

_____

4. _____

_____

5. _____

_____

6. _____

_____

7. _____

_____

8. _____

_____

9. _____

_____

10. _____

_____

# Appendix C

Parent Questionnaire

1.  Do I communicate with my children concerning having a good day at school?
2.  What kind of attitude do I have when I communicate with my children?
3.  Am I a good provider for my children?
4.  In planning my day, am I able to have a time of inspiration with my children?
5.  Do I have a quiet time daily for myself?
6.  Am I spending daily quality time with each of my children?
7.  During the homework period, do you manage control when you get frustrated with your children?
8.  Do you see your children as a joy or a burden?
9.  Were you the best parent you could be today?
10. Do you compare your children, or do you treat them as individuals?
11. At any time did I feel the need to apologize to my children?

# About the Author

Catherine Smith Robinson is a minister, educator, author, poet, consultant, and program designer. She is a native of Atlanta, and holds a master's degree in education. Her unique style of parent involvement has successfully educated all levels of youth and children for almost fifty years. She received the Eagles' Award for her outstanding service in the field of teaching.

Ms. Robinson is the founder and CEO of Save Our Children (SOC) Inc., and Healing and Restoration Inc. She also started her own radio broadcast as an outreach to the community and other states, to teach the importance of parenting. Her partnership with the Mayor's Office of Community Affairs under the leadership of Mayor Bill Campbell assisted her with the success of major projects in drug prevention in high-risk schools and communities. Programs were designed by Ms. Robinson to build resilient children in an effort to decrease drug use in children. Several governors in Georgia recognized SOC for outstanding achievement in drug prevention.

In keeping with her purpose, she started a family ministry on behalf of the children—"The Princesses and Princes"—focusing on the celebration of their identity according to godly principles. She participates in the social media network ministry as a minister for "Healing Hearts," focused on healing and restoration, and "Save Our Children Mission." Ms. Robinson is the Bible teacher for "Rise and be Healed," a weekly senior community ministry.

Catherine Smith Robinson, MEd
healourchildren@gmail.com

Printed in the United States
By Bookmasters